AFP World News Report 5

— Achieving the Sustainable Development Goals (SDGs)—

AFPニュースで見る世界 5

Makoto Shishido

Kevin Murphy

Mariko Takahashi

photographs by

AFP＝時事／iStockphoto

DVD / Streaming Materials

LESSON 1: © AFP/NASHWA GOWANLOCK, RAPHAEL AMBASU

LESSON 2: © AFP/DIANA CHAN, GLENDA KWEK

LESSON 3: © AFP/DIANE DESOBEAU

LESSON 4: © AFP/RAPHAEL AMBASU

LESSON 5: © AFP/SÉBASTIEN VUAGNAT, KATE GILLAM, KATIE SCHUBAUER

LESSON 6: © AFP/MARYKE VERMAAK, AMY GIBBINGS

LESSON 7: © AFP/WWF/VOLANA RAZAFIMANANTSOA

LESSON 8: © AFP/PHYO HEIN KYAW, JUSTINE GERARDY

LESSON 9: © AFP/WILLIAM EDWARDS

LESSON 10: © AFP/RICHARD SARGENT/JEANNE HALLACY/ EQUALITY MYANMA

LESSON 11: © AFP/NAIRA DAVLASHYAN, REZA NOURMAMODE, EKATERINA ANISIMOVA, ANDREI BORODULIN

LESSON 12: © AFP/STRINGER, EMILY IRVING-SWIFT

LESSON 13: © AFP/DAPHNÉE DENIS, VALERIA PACHECO, CARLOS REYES

LESSON 14: © AFP/GIANRIGO MARLETTA

LESSON 15: © AFP/GIANRIGO MARLETTA

LESSON 16: © AFP/JONATHAN KLEIN

StreamLine

Web 動画・音声ファイルのストリーミング再生について

CD マーク及び Web 動画マークがある箇所は、PC、スマートフォン、タブレット端末において、無料でストリーミング再生することができます。下記 URL よりご利用ください。再生手順や動作環境などは本書巻末の「Web 動画のご案内」をご覧ください。

http://st.seibido.co.jp

音声ファイルのダウンロードについて

CD マークがある箇所は、ダウンロードすることも可能です。下記 URL より書籍を検索し、書籍詳細ページにあるダウンロードアイコンをクリックしてください。

https://www.seibido.co.jp

AFP World News Report 5
— Achieving the Sustainable Development Goals (SDGs)—

はじめに

　本書は、国際連合 (United Nations) が提案している持続可能な開発目標 Sustainable Development Goals の 17 項目の目標から 16 項目を取り上げ、それぞれの目標に関しての最新の情報を知ること、目標を達成するために学生自身が、何ができるかを考えることを主眼としております。
持続可能な開発目標のそれぞれの項目に関連した AFP World Academic Archive の映像ニュースを取り上げ、目標に関連したニュースのリスニング、英文読解を通じて、初中級レベルの英語力を養成することを目的としています。英語を聞き、理解する力、英文を読み、内容を理解する力、各課の目標項目について、自らできる行動を考え、意見をまとめ、発表をする力を養成するために必要と考える練習問題を、さまざまな工夫を凝らし、配列しています。
最近注目されている持続可能な開発目標に関連する AFP のニュース映像と、読みやすい英文を利用し、基礎的な英語理解力を高めるとともに、英語を聴く力、読む力、意見を述べる力を養成することを主眼とした、初中級者向けの教材です。
本書の構成は下記のような特徴を持っています。

　1. Listening は、AFP WAA のニュース映像を各課の話題への導入として利用しています。学生に各課のテーマについて興味を持たせる役割を持っています。

　1. **Key Word Study** は、ニュース映像に出てくる基礎的な重要単語を学ぶことで、話題への理解と単語力の強化を目指します。
　2. **Listening Practice – First Viewing** は、ニュース映像の全体像を理解するための T/F 形式の問題です。
　3. **Listening Practice 2** は、細かな音の聞き取りを確認するディクテーションの問題です。
　4. **Comprehension Check – Second Viewing** は、さらに詳細な内容を理解しているか確認するための練習問題です。
　5. **Summary** は、映像で紹介されたニュースの要旨を理解しているか、最終的に確認する問題です。音声を聞き、空所を補充する形式となっています。

　2. Reading は、英文読解を通じて各課のニュース映像で紹介された持続可能な開発目標の内容を展開させ、さまざまな意見を紹介するものです。この英文は中心となる話題や意見の提示で、比較的容易に英語で書かれた 250 ～ 260 語程度の英文読解です。持続可能な開発目標に関する情報を読むばかりでなく、基本的な英語力、単語力、読解力、思考力を身につけることを目指しています。

　1. **Vocabulary Check** は、英文の中で取り上げられている基礎的な英単語の学習です。
　2. **Comprehension Questions** は、英文の内容理解を問う問題です。学生が自ら英語で答える形式の問になっています。
　3. **Grammar Check** は、基本的な文法事項の確認を兼ねた語順整序演習です。

　3. Discussion では、学生が積極的に参加する対話型講義への展開として、批判的思考に基づいた学生の意見を発表させることを目指しております。国際連合の持続可能な開発目標を達成するための 170 のアクションの中から抜粋した、各課で提示される目標を達成するために自らできることを選び、個々の学生による発表、討論など指導者の裁量でさまざまな展開が可能であると考えます。

　以上 3 部のさまざまな練習問題から、現代社会で話題となっていることがらについて英語で考えながら、単語力、聴解力、読解力、文法理解力、発話力、討論力など総合的な英語能力の養成に役立つでしょう。本書を活用し、英語力の一層の向上と、社会におけるさまざまな最新情報に対する正しい理解が図られ、健全な社会生活を送るための一助となることを願います。

　なお、スクリプト、英文の注釈等には細心の注意を払って作成いたしましたが、お気づきの点がございましたらご教授いただければ幸いです。

　最後になりましたが、本書の編集、出版にあたり、ひとかたならぬご尽力を賜った㈱成美堂、工藤隆志氏、萩原美奈子氏に心より感謝申し上げます。

出典：About the Sustainable Development Goals
　　　https://www.un.org/sustainabledevelopment/sustainable-development-goals/
　　　170 Actions to Transform Our World
　　　https://drive.google.com/file/d/1iMdE6DLLuCqwq3K9U-DaTUWB6KyMa8QG/view

2019 年 7 月

著者一同

CONTENTS

SUSTAINABLE DEVELOPMENT G◎ALS

1 NO POVERTY | **2 ZERO HUNGER** | **3 GOOD HEALTH AND WELL-BEING** | **4 QUALITY EDUCATION** | **5 GENDER EQUALITY** | **6 CLEAN WATER AND SANITATION**

7 AFFORDABLE AND CLEAN ENERGY | **8 DECENT WORK AND ECONOMIC GROWTH** | **9 INDUSTRY, INNOVATION AND INFRASTRUCTURE** | **10 REDUCED INEQUALITIES** | **11 SUSTAINABLE CITIES AND COMMUNITIES** | **12 RESPONSIBLE CONSUMPTION AND PRODUCTION**

13 CLIMATE ACTION | **14 LIFE BELOW WATER** | **15 LIFE ON LAND** | **16 PEACE, JUSTICE AND STRONG INSTITUTIONS** | **17 PARTNERSHIPS FOR THE GOALS**

No Poverty

Donate what you don't use

　世界では７億人以上、全人口の 11%が貧困に苦しみ、健康的な生活を送ること、教育を受けること、飲料水を入手すること、衛生設備の完備した暮らしができていません。これらの問題を解決するためにあなたは何ができますか。

I LISTENING

I Key Word Study | *Before Watching the Video*

Match each word with its definition.

1. advertise	( )	2. dare	( )	3. drive	( )
4. feature	( )	5. inspiration	( )	6. mentor	( )
7. orphaned	( )	8. pursue	( )	9. spill	( )
10. venture into	( )				

> a. 危険を冒して〜する　　b. 衝動　　c. 広告する　　d. ばらす　　e. 良き助言者
> f. 鼓舞させること　　g. 特集する　　h. 追う　　i. 孤児になる　　j. 冒険的に試みる

2 Listening Practice 1 | *First Viewing*　　　　　(Time 01:54) WEB動画 🖥 💿DVD

Watch the news clip and write T if the statement is true or F if it is false.

1. Henry Ohanga grew up in one of the largest cities in Africa. ( )
2. Octopizzo wants to help young people realize their dreams. ( )
3. His songs became hits and he was being featured on major advertising campaigns. ( )
4. Daniel Owino only works as a hip-hop singer. ( )
5. Owino has not recorded any songs yet. ( )

Listen to the recording and fill in the missing words.

Narrator : Kibera, one of Africa's largest slums and the place where Henry Ohanga grew up. Orphaned by the age of 15, he ended up joining a gang before turning his life around. Today, he's known as Octopizzo, the "octo" a reference to the only bus line that dares venture into this neighborhood. And now he wants to help young people realize they too can make a name for themselves.

Kibera ケニア共和国首都ナイロビの一地域
Henry Ohanga (Octopizzo) Kibera 地区出身の音楽家

make a name for oneself 有名になる

Octopizzo : I want to be like the face of possibility because when you grow up here you are told [1](   ) (   ) (   ) (   ) (   ). You are told this by your teacher in school, you are told this by your dad probably at home, and most of the time it starts hitting you and you realize — ooh I will never be anything anyway.

Narrator : During the 2007 post-election violence, his anger spilled into his first recorded song, "Voices of Kibera." It wasn't long before [2](   ) (   ) (   ) (   ) and he was being featured on major advertising campaigns. Kibera, where most of his family and friends still live, remains close to his heart and features in every one of his hits.

2007 post-election violence ケニア危機（ケニアで2007年12月27日から2008年2月28日までに起きた暴動とそれによって叫ばれた政治危機）

Octopizzo : I feel like if I was not born here I would probably not be a rapper. [3](   ) (   ) (   ) (   ) (   ). I probably won't have the same drive.

Narrator : And in Kibera, his musical career is an inspiration. Former "bad kid" Daniel Owino and Octopizzo fan

now [4](   ) (   ) (   )
(   ) (   ) (   ) while
pursuing his passion for hip-hop.

Daniel Owino : When I saw that boy now, who is living larger
than life, I felt like [5](   ) (   )
(   ) (   ) (   )
(   ) one day. Because we were with
Octopizzo just down here in the slum.

Narrator : Thanks to Octopizzo, Owino has already recorded 13
songs. And meanwhile his mentor is recording a new
album.

---

4 | Comprehension Check   *Second Viewing*

Watch the news clip again and answer the following questions in English.

1. What did Henry Ohanga do before becoming a rap singer?

   ....

2. Why does Octopizzo visit his home town?

   ....

3. What are the students in Kibera told by their teachers?

   ....

4. Where do most of Octopizzo's family and friends still live?

   ....

5. What is Octopizzo doing now?

   ....

5 | Summary   1-04

Listen to the recording and complete the summary.

One of east Africa's most popular hip-hop stars, Octopizzo, is using his [1](   )
to break down stigma around the slum he grew up in and inspire kids in a world
devoid of successful role models. Former "bad kid" Daniel Owino now works as a
motorbike taxi driver while [2](   ) his passion for hip-hop. He has already
recorded 13 songs while his [3](   ) is recording a new album.

❚❚ READING 1-05

   The year 2030 will be an important milestone for the United Nations. By this date, the UN plans to increase living standards for all those at the lower end of the poverty scale and come close to ending extreme poverty around the world.

   How this milestone will be achieved is uncertain and relies on the goodwill
5 of those in power. While a focus on living standards can bring about change for some, the UN wants increased support in education and social protection for all. By doing this it hopes to impact extreme poverty in two ways. Firstly, it wants to raise the number of people in stable employment. Large numbers of people, particularly young women, are in low-paid, insecure work. Inequality in education is one reason
10 for this. Low levels of public funding and gender inequalities have resulted in many people receiving only a minimal education. As a result, many of the poorest have only temporary or seasonal work and no steady income. Secondly, the UN stresses the importance of social protection. It believes that all workers should have help with family or home issues. When workers can more easily adjust to new situations, they
15 often become more productive. To achieve this, they must have access to a system that supports them through hard times. Without this support, many workers are unable to pay for basic needs when sick or in times of crisis, and their families suffer.

   Changing the situation of those who are often excluded is not an easy thing to do. However, the UN believes that social policies which favor the poorest members of
20 society can change lives and may bring their 2030 goal within reach.   (280 words)

Notes
milestone 画期的な出来事 **goodwill** 善意 **minimal** 最小の

1 | Vocabulary Check

Fill in the blanks with the most appropriate words from the list below.

1. (   ) speaking is an important business skill.

2. Global warming has caused (   ) weather conditions.

3. This advertisement is on (   ) display.

4. The staff had to (   ) the position of the picture.

5. Students should study hard to (   ) a good grade.

> extreme   achieve   public   temporary   adjust

10

2 | Comprehension Questions

Answer the following questions in English.

1. What year will be an important milestone for the United Nations?

    ....

2. What is the first thing the UN is going to do to impact extreme poverty?

    ....

3. Why are many people receiving only a minimal education?

    ....

4. What is the second thing the UN is going to do to impact extreme poverty?

    ....

5. How can workers more easily adjust to new situations?

    ....

3 | Grammar Check

Unscramble the following words and complete the sentences.

1. [study, is, while, to, it, hard, important, for] a test, it is also important to sleep well before the test.

    .... a test, it is also important to sleep well before the test.

2. [English, books, reading, many, by, in], Maki's reading skill has dramatically improved.

    ...., Maki's reading skill has dramatically improved.

3. [game, who, purchase, those, the, to, want, new] should line up in front of the shop.

    .... should line up in front of the shop.

 **DISCUSSION**

Goal 1: NO POVERTY
Why it matters

もし世界規模で健康と教育の改善がなされなければ、2030年までに1億6700万人の子どもたちが極度の貧困状態で生活することになると予測されています。そのような状況を避けるため、以下の目標が挙げられています。

Goal	To end poverty in all its forms everywhere by 2030. （2030年までに、すべての地域であらゆる貧困を撲滅する）

この目標を達成するために、私たちは何ができるでしょうか？　以下に挙げる例から自分ができると思う行動を1つ選び、その理由をクラスで発表しましょう。

Daily actions you may want to take:

1. Get everyone involved. Have a class do regular outreach day trips to areas in need.

2. Buy fair-trade products to support a sustainable trade system, meaning employees are rewarded fairly for their work.

3. Teach a skill or short course at a community center (computer skills, building a resume, preparing for job interviews).

4. Buy clothing or other products from stores that donate a portion of their money to charities.

5. Clean out your pantry. Fill a box with non-perishable foods and donate it to a food bank.

6. Generate discussion around poverty. Write a blog or write an article in a local newspaper.

番号：＿＿＿＿＿＿

理由	
具体的な行動	

Avoid throwing away food

　飢餓と栄養失調は、持続可能な開発の障壁となっています。現在全世界で7億9500万人が飢餓に苦しんでいます。飢餓は、簡単には脱することができない落とし穴でもあります。飢餓と栄養失調により、生産性も低下します。飢餓をゼロにするためにあなたは何ができますか。

❶ LISTENING

1 | Key Word Study | *Before Watching the Video*

Match each word with its definition.

1. ambitious ( )　　2. appetite ( )　　3. collaborate ( )

4. donate ( )　　5. landfill ( )　　6. optimistic ( )

7. rack up ( )　　8. reject ( )　　9. stock with ( )

10. tighten ( )

a. 寄付する	b. 欲求	c. 〜を仕入れる	d.（埋め立て式）ごみ処理地
e. 厳しくする	f. 楽観的な	g. 〜をあげる	h. 意欲的な	i. 拒絶する
j. 協力する			

2 | Listening Practice 1 | *First Viewing*　　　　　(Time 02:20) WEB動画 🖥💿 DVD

Watch the news clip and write T if the statement is true or F if it is false.

1. Australia's first recycled supermarket gives away groceries for free. ( )
2. Australia doesn't produce enough food for its population. ( )
3. The Australian government aims to cut food waste in half by 2030. ( )
4. Annabel Stewart thinks using plastic for food packaging is good. ( )
5. Half of the food produced in the world is lost or wasted. ( )

3 | Listening Practice 2

WEB動画 DVD CD 1-07

Listen to the recording and fill in the missing words.

Narrator: Fighting food waste, one bite at a time. Australia's first "recycled" supermarket gives away groceries for free. It's stocked with food from shops, airlines and other suppliers that would otherwise end up in a landfill.

Fiona Ngarn: We've got a few different types, shepherd's pie, we've got a curry, we've got a black-bean stir-fry, ¹(   ) (   ) (   ) (   ), which is good if you're either feeding yourself or feeding a family.

Narrator: Australia has a population of 24 million, but produces enough food for almost three times that number. Even so, hundreds of thousands ²(   ) (   ) (   ) (   ) to fill their stomachs. Ronni Kahn, founder of OzHarvest, hopes the supermarket will not only feed the needy but also educate people about sustainable living.

Ronni Kahn: There are definitely people who are coming who are in need who this is a lifesaver for them. And then there are people who want to take part in this sharing

economy and who want to feel that they are taking produce or buying produce because ³(   ) (   ) (   ) (   ) (   ) (   ) to OzHarvest, taking produce and understanding why this produce was rejected.

Narrator: The government aims to halve food waste by 2030, ⁴(   ) (   ) (   ) (   ) (   ) (   ) (   )

shepherd's pie シェパーズパイ (マッシュポテトで作るパイ皮と牛肉 (または羊肉) で作るイギリスのミートパイ)
black-bean stir-fry 炒めた黒インゲン豆

OzHarvest オーストラリアの食糧救済慈善団体
the needy 貧困者
sustainable living 持続可能な生活

14

NGOs and the private sector to tighten wastage from paddock to plate. But workers at the supermarket are already looking beyond simply saving food.

paddock 牧場

Annabel Stewart: So even with us rescuing all this food, you look at a different angle and you look, there's plastic everywhere. Plastic, plastic in carrots, in all of this stuff, herbs,

so even though we are doing a good thing, there's more to be done for sure.

Narrator: [5](   ) (   ) (   ) (   ) (   ) produced in the world is lost or wasted, racking up to 1 trillion US dollars in cost every year. But as the government steps up its war against food waste, supporters are optimistic about Australia's appetite for change.

1 trillion US dollars 一兆米ドル

---

4 | Comprehension Check   *Second Viewing*

WEB動画   DVD

Watch the news clip again and answer the following questions in English.

1. From where does the supermarket get its stocks of food?

   ....

2. What does Ronni Kahn hope the supermarket will do?

   ....

3. Who are the people who buy products at the supermarket?

   ....

4. Who does the government collaborate with to reduce waste?

   ....

5. What is the value of the food lost or wasted in the world?

   ....

5 | Summary

Listen to the recording and complete the summary.

Australia's first "recycled" supermarket is giving food ¹(   ) for landfills a second chance, as the government embarks on a major push to cut down on ²(   ) costing the economy Aus\$20 billion a year. A third of the food produced in the world is lost or wasted, ³(   ) up to 1 trillion US dollars in cost every year.

▮▮ READING

 1-09

  Approximately one third of all food produced in the world is thrown away, wasted, or lost. There are a number of reasons for this, but it is tragic that as food is left unused, millions go hungry. Data shows that the hungriest people live in Asia, and while over 500 million people are undernourished, Asian countries now account

5 for more than 50 percent of global food wastage.

  Perhaps surprisingly, this is not just a problem for the consumer. Food loss and food waste are not the same thing. Food loss refers to food that is spoiled or lost before arriving at the market. Producing, harvesting, or storing can all cause problems before any food reaches the shelves. In the UK, food is left to rot in fields due to the

10 lack of farm workers able to pick the crops. In India, the problem is a lack of storage. In China, much of the loss is from issues with transport and distribution.

  Food waste, on the other hand, refers to food that is lost after reaching the household, restaurant or supermarket. In Japan, for example, it is estimated that over 6 million tons of food is wasted in these sectors every year. The choosy nature of

15 consumers has led to over-production in order to satisfy their need for choice, and a lack of facilities means still edible food is thrown into landfill sites. This food may just as easily be sent to recycling centers for redistribution.

  The current situation suggests it may take more effort from law makers to halt the upward trends of loss and waste and so better assist the world's hungry.

(273 words)

Notes

undernourished 栄養不良の

1 Vocabulary Check

Fill in the blanks with the most appropriate words from the list below.

1. English is used as a (   ) language.

2. (   ) have the right to know the ingredients of processed food.

3. Scholars have (   ) the number of household pets in some countries.

4. Thomas failed an easy quiz because of (   ) of sleep.

5. Sabrina did not wait for the others because she did not want to (   )
   time.

> waste   global   consumers   lack   estimated

2 Comprehension Questions

Answer the following questions in English.

1. What proportion of food produced in the world is thrown away?

   ....

2. Where do the hungriest people live?

   ....

3. What does food loss refer to?

   ....

4. What does food waste refer to?

   ....

5. How much food is wasted in Japan every year?

   ....

3 Grammar Check

Unscramble the following words and complete the sentences.

1. [have, we, is, that, annoying, to, it] fill in the form every time.

   .... fill in the form every time.

2. David had to spend a night at the airport [his, to, late, arrival, due, of, flight, the].

   David had to spend a night at the airport ....

3. Kate practices the piano very hard [order, mother, satisfy, to, her, in].

   Kate practices the piano very hard ....

Goal 2 : ZERO HUNGER
Why it matters

今日の 7 億 9,500 万人の飢餓に苦しむ人々と、2050 年までに人口増加が見込まれるさらなる 20 億人に十分な食料を供給するために、世界の食料と農業システムを大きく変えることが必要です。そのため、以下の目標が挙げられています。

Goal	To end hunger, achieve food security and improved nutrition and promote sustainable agriculture. (飢餓を撲滅し、食料の保障と栄養の改善を達成し、持続可能な農業を推進する)

この目標を達成するために、私たちに何ができるでしょうか？　以下に挙げる例から自分ができると思う行動を 1 つ選び、その理由をクラスで発表しましょう。

Daily actions you may want to take:

1. Spread the word. The more ideas are spread to combat hunger, the more people act.
2. Donate non-perishable foods to charities.
3. Support food assistance programs. They provide over 20 times more food than food banks, food pantries, and soup kitchens.
4. Many emergency food providers need specialized skills such as accounting, social media, or writing skills. Volunteer your expertise once a week.
5. Read a book on hunger. A greater understanding of its causes will better prepare you to make a difference.
6. Support local farmers by buying your food at farmers' markets.

番号：＿＿＿＿＿

理由	
具体的な行動	

LESSON 3

Good Health & Well-being

Vaccinate your family to protect them and improve public health

　すべての人に健康と福祉を提供することは、繁栄する社会を築く上でとても重要です。毎年 10 億ドルの予防接種のための予算があれば、100 万人の子供を救うことができます。人々に健康をもたらすためにあなたは何ができますか。

I LISTENING

I | Key Word Study | *Before Watching the Video*

Match each word with its definition.

1. accuse of	( )	2. diagnose	( )	3. infertility	( )
4. ingredient	( )	5. initiative	( )	6. paralyze	( )
7. prevent	( )	8. prohibit	( )	9. refusal	( )
10. tangible	( )				

a. 拒否	b. 明白な	c. 非難する	d. 成分	e. 予防する
f. 診断する	g. 不妊	h. 禁止する	i. 取り組み	j. まひさせる

2 | Listening Practice 1 | *First Viewing*　　　(Time 02:28) 🖥 WEB動画 💿 DVD

Watch the news clip and write T if the statement is true or F if it is false.

1. Pakistan is the only country in the world where polio remains endemic. (　)
2. Many Pakistani parents believe the vaccine may cause infertility. (　)
3. The vaccinators are often accused of being thieves. (　)
4. The campaigners in Karachi started hiring local women to dispel the doubts. (　)
5. No cases of polio have been reported in Pakistan since the beginning of the year. (　)

Listen to the recording and fill in the missing words.

Narrator : Knocking on their neighbors' doors with a mission—eradicating polio. Pakistan is one of only two countries in the world—along with Afghanistan—where the crippling disease remains endemic. [1](   ) (   ) (   ) (   ) (   ) is to vaccinate children under five, but it's not that easy. On this door—an "R" for refusal, meaning the youngsters living here did not get the necessary dose last month.

eradicate 根絶する

polio ポリオ (小児まひ)

crippling disease 大きな障害を与える病気
endemic 地方病

dose 服用量

Rabia: We don't give the vaccine because we're afraid that our children will become disabled.

disabled 身体障害になった

Narrator : Despite her fears, Rabia lets her children be treated this time—[2](   ) (   ) (   ) (   ) (   ) (   ) by her neighbors. But her concerns are shared by many Pakistani parents, who also believe the vaccine can cause infertility or contains ingredients prohibited by Islam. The vaccinators themselves are often accused of being spies, since the CIA used a fake polio campaign to track down Osama Bin Laden five years ago. To dispel such doubts, campaigners in Karachi started hiring local women like Sharmeen in 2014.

dispel 追い散らす

Sharmeen Aslam: As I am local, I can tell them that if the vaccine does any harm to their children, [3](   ) (   ) (   ) (   ) (   ). So they think that because I am living here, they can just come to my home if there is any problem.

Narrator : And the results are tangible—the number of refusals fell by three quarters last year. Another reason for the initiative: security. Since 2012, a hundred people have been killed in attacks targeting vaccination campaigns —including three in this neighborhood in 2014. At the time, [4](   ) (   ) (   ) (   ) (   ) (   )—and a shortage of police officers regularly prevented them from doing their job. But things are different with neighborhood vaccinators.

Asif Hyder Shah: They know people around there, so they feel [5](   ) (   ) (   ) (   ) (   ) (   ) also. So in those areas, we do not have police following every team, but the entry and exit points are covered.

Narrator : But for Mohammad, it's too late. This 18 month-old boy missed part of the vaccination and was diagnosed with polio last December. His right foot is paralyzed— and his family doesn't know if he'll ever be able to walk. Five other cases have been reported in Pakistan since the beginning of the year—a stark reminder of the dangers that still exist for Mohammad's young neighbors.

paralyzed	麻痺させられた
stark	ありのままの

---

4 | Comprehension Check   *Second Viewing*   WEB動画 💻 📀 DVD

Watch the news clip again and answer the following questions in English.

1. What is the aim of the women knocking on their neighbors' doors?

   ....

2. Why do many Pakistani mothers refuse to allow their children to be vaccinated?

   ....

3. What did the CIA do five years ago?

   ....

4. How did the number of refusals change after campaigners hired local women last year?

   ....

5.   What is Mohammad's family unsure of?

....

Listen to the recording and complete the summary.

In a rundown district of Karachi, one mother balks at a neighbor's [1](   )
to vaccinate her children, demonstrating one of the biggest hurdles to eradicating
polio in Pakistan by the end of the year: [2](   ) and frightened parents.
Many Pakistani parents believe the vaccine can cause [3](   ) or contains
ingredients prohibited by Islam.

II READING 1-13

The World Health Organization defines health as a state of complete well-being,
separate from a lack of sickness or the ailments that come with old age. They specify
three factors that can help reduce the threats to health. These threats can include
deaths in childbirth or transferable diseases, the rate of self-harm or substance abuse.

5   The first factor involves good physical health through vaccination programs. The
UN argues that these can save up to three million lives a year, keep workers healthy,
and prevent families from falling into poverty. It is reported that the mortality rate
of under five-year-olds may be reduced with access to the correct medicines and
nutrition. In these cases, health programs will greatly improve and protect the quality
10   of life for those who are vulnerable.

The second factor covers good mental health. The UN maintains that illnesses
develop at a young age. If left untreated they can lead to depression, a major cause of
illness for young people. This in turn can affect education levels and is also linked
to cases of suicide. Treating mental illnesses is a long-term benefit as it provides a
15   happier, more stable workforce.

The final factor involves good social health. The UN wants governments to create
better public health systems that allow people to make the right choices for children
and families. By understanding the threats they face, people are more able to obtain
care when it is most needed.

20   Ensuring that all people have access to vaccines, are stress-free, and have a health
system that provides extensive basic care is a key goal of the UN. Used in the right
areas, these programs are life changing.   (275 words)

1 Vocabulary Check

Fill in the blanks with the most appropriate words from the list below.

1. Generation Z is (   ) as those who were born after 2000.

2. More than 20 people are (   ) in this project.

3. It was (   ) that the company successfully developed a new medicine.

4. Automobile manufacturing has been a (   ) industry in Japan.

5. The university has an (   ) program for exchange students.

major   extensive   defined   reported   involved

2 Comprehension Questions

Answer the following questions in English.

1. How is health defined by the World Health Organization?

   ....

2. How many people does the UN argue can be saved by vaccination programs?

   ....

3. What can depression affect?

   ....

4. Why is treating mental illness considered a long-term benefit?

   ....

5. What does the UN want governments to do?

   ....

3 Grammar Check

Unscramble the following words and complete the sentences.

1. The shop sells [things, ranging, computers, various, from, to] bicycles.

   The shop sells .... bicycles.

2. 5G [us, with, communicate, allows, to, others] faster than ever.

   5G .... faster than ever.

3. A strong storm [from, flying, plane, the, prevented, to] the original destination.

   A strong storm .... the original destination.

Goal 3: GOOD HEALTH AND WELL-BEING
Why it matters

予防接種に 10 億ドルを費やすことで、毎年 100 万人の子供の命を救うことができます。その
ため、以下の目標が挙げられています。

Goal	To ensure healthy lives and promote well-being for all at all ages. （すべての年齢の、すべての人々のために、健康的な生活を保障し、幸福を促進する）

この目標を達成するために、私たちに何ができるでしょうか？　以下に挙げる例から自分
ができると思う行動を 1 つ選び、その理由をクラスで発表しましょう。

Daily actions you may want to take:

1. Don't smoke.
2. Be more active. Go for walks at lunchtime or cycle to work.
3. Eat a healthy diet and drink a lot of water.
4. HIV/AIDS is not over. Protect yourself. Test yourself.
5. Get enough sleep.
6. Make time for yourself and your friends.

番号：＿＿＿＿＿

理由	
具体的な行動	

LESSON 4

Quality Education

Help children in your community to read

　教育は、持続可能な開発目標を達成するために最も有効な手段です。発展途上国では、91%の子供が教育を受けていますが、5700万人の子供は、いまだに学校に通えていません。質の高い教育をあらゆる人に提供するために、あなたは何ができますか。

I LISTENING

1 Key Word Study | *Before Watching the Video*

Match each word with its definition.

1. alternative （　） 　　2. decade 　　（　） 　　3. destitute 　　（　）

4. famine 　　（　） 　　5. flee 　　（　） 　　6. literacy 　　（　）

7. makeshift 　（　） 　　8. numeracy 　（　） 　　9. refugee 　　（　）

10. uproot 　　（　）

a. 読み書き能力	b. 難民	c. 間に合わせの	d. 追い立てる	e. 貧しい
f. ～の代わり	g. 食糧不足	h. 10年間	i. ～から逃げる	
j. 数学の基礎知識があること				

2 Listening Practice 1 | *First Viewing*　　　　(Time 02:00) WEB動画 DVD

Watch the news clip and write T if the statement is true or F if it is false.

1. Young teachers are teaching basic literacy and numeracy skills. 　　（　）

2. Hasno wants to be a nurse to help people in hospitals. 　　（　）

3. The volunteers teach nearly 6,000 students in five refugee camps. 　　（　）

4. The students are aged between six and 18. 　　（　）

5. Decades of civil war and famine have led hundreds of thousands of
   Somalis to flee their homes. 　　（　）

Listen to the recording and fill in the missing words.

Narrator: Uprooted from their homes by war and famine, these children are finally back in the classroom. For years, they've been living with their families in IDP camps outside Mogadishu ¹(   ) (   ) (   ) (   ). Young student volunteers are teaching them basic literacy and numeracy skills under makeshift shelters, sometimes just under a tree.

IDP 国内避難民

Mogadishu ソマリアの首都

Abdirashid Abdullahi: At first we could not even feed them, but at least we can teach them ²(   ) (   ) (   ) (   ) (   ) (   ).

Narrator: The volunteers teach nearly 600 students aged between six and 15 in four refugee camps near the capital.

Hasno: I like studying in this school and later, I want to be a nurse to help people in hospitals.

Narrator: Without resources, families cannot afford to send their children to school. ³(   ) (   ) (   ) (   ) (   ) (   ) (   ) offer an alternative to Koranic schools, which are the only other source of free education.

Koranic school イスラム教国の民衆の初等教育機関

Maka Sheikh Isaq: These volunteers give classes to many of my children, because I cannot pay school fees. Before, I did everything I could to get two of my sons to go to school, ⁴(   ) (   ) (   ) (   ) (   ) (   ) (   ) . I have other children and I cannot

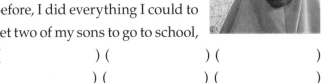

pay for school.

Narrator: Decades of civil war and famine have led hundreds of thousands of Somalis to flee their homes and
5(   ) (   )
(   ) (   )
(   ). It's hoped the initiative will help some of the country's most destitute children to dream of a better future than their parents.

Somalis ソマリ人

-----

4 | Comprehension Check   *Second Viewing*

Watch the news clip again and answer the following questions in English.

1. Where have the children been living?

   ....

2. Where do young student volunteers teach?

   ....

3. What are Koranic schools?

   ....

4. How much did it cost for Maka Sheikh Isaq to send two of her sons to school?

   ....

5. What is it hoped the initiative will help?

   ....

   ....

5 | Summary   1-16

Listen to the recording and complete the summary.

Ravaged by decades of war, Somalia has one of the lowest 1(   ) rates in the world. Successive governments, busy managing political crises and the threat of terrorism, have 2(   ) the field of education. Today, people who have fled their area and live in IDP camps are often not able to send their children to school, but citizen 3(   ) are changing that.

Education is a human right. Since 1948, countries around the world have agreed that it should be available to all in some form or
5   other. The reasons for this consensus reflect on both the individual and wider society.

For the individual, the United Nations emphasizes the role of self-
10 esteem. Education gives a person the skill to understand and make their way in the world. It is a vital part of how we think about and see ourselves in society. When a person is given an education, they have more pride. With pride, all human beings are valued as contributing members of a community. They appreciate that respect should be shown to others and that they
15 should act in a manner that does no harm.

In wider society, education is important to nurture the personality of each person. In order to deal with family, friends, and social groups, a person needs the ability to connect with and know what others value. In recent years, this also entails communicating through the use of technology. Education is a key means of learning
20 the culture and values of a social group. It ensures that those things that are valued are continued. It can also inspire and promote all areas of society, whether it is building a national identity, advocating for justice, or fighting inequality.

To contribute to society, a person needs to know who they are and understand how to treat and relate to others. This is learned through education. Without this
25 understanding, human beings may lack the pride or the ability to play an active and informed role in their society.

(270 words)

Notes
self-esteem 自尊心   **vital** 不可欠な

1 | Vocabulary Check

Fill in the blanks with the most appropriate words from the list below.

1. People (   ) the right of free speech.

2. The event (   ) Peter to begin a new experiment.

3. The group has been (   ) for animal rights.

4. Jessica is an (   ) member of a volunteering club.

5. The new technology will soon become (   ) to everyone.

> available   appreciate   advocating   inspired   active

2 | Comprehension Questions

Answer the following questions in English.

1. Since when have countries agreed education should be available to all?

   ....

2. What skill does education give a person?

   ....

3. Why is education important in wider society?

   ....

4. What is education a key means of?

   ....

5. What do people need to know to contribute to society?

   ....

3 | Grammar Check

Unscramble the following words and complete the sentences.

1. Our culture affects [the, look, we, world, at, how].

   Our culture affects ....

2. Fragile items [be, caution, treated, should, with].

   Fragile items ....

3. Governments have to consider everyone, [infrastructure, developing, they, or, are, planning, whether] health care systems.

   Governments have to consider everyone, ...

   .... health care systems.

Goal 4: QUALITY EDUCATION
Why it matters

発展途上国の初等教育への受講は91%に達していますが、5,700万人の子供たちが学校に行けないままです。そのような状況を避けるため、以下の目標が挙げられています。

Goal	Ensure inclusive and quality education for all and promote lifelong learning. (すべての人が参加する、質の高い教育を確実にし、生涯学習を促進する)

この目標を達成するために、私たちに何ができるでしょうか？　以下に挙げる例から自分ができると思う行動を1つ選び、その理由をクラスで発表しましょう。

Daily actions you may want to take:

1. Teach your native language to migrants in a youth center or elsewhere.
2. Educate your kids about the power of education as many don't see the tangible benefits.
3. Support charities that are working in education in the poorest parts of the world.
4. Donate books to public libraries or public schools in need.
5. Share your skills with the ones who need them.
6. In many countries, girls are pulled out of school early in order to get married. Start conversations that allow for problems to be openly discussed and solutions to be found.

番号：_____

理由	
具体的な行動	

LESSON 5 — Gender Equality

Call out sexist language and behavior

管理職や経営者となっている女性は、平均で3分の1以下にとどまっています。女性は世界の人口の半分です。男女間の不平等が、社会の発展を妨げています。ジェンダー平等を実現するために、あなたは何ができますか。

① LISTENING

1 | Key Word Study | *Before Watching the Video*

Match each word with its definition.

1. ally	( )	2. diversity	( )	3. embark	( )
4. evident	( )	5. exception	( )	6. hesitant	( )
7. nominate	( )	8. norm	(.)	9. reflect	( )
10. substantial	( )				

a. ためらいがちな	b. 着手する	c. 反映する	d. 明らかな
e. 指名する	f. しっかりした	g. 多様性	h. 例外
i. 標準	j. 味方		

2 | Listening Practice 1 | *First Viewing* (Time 02:17) WEB動画 🖳 DVD

Watch the news clip and write T if the statement is true or F if it is false.

1. Liz Holland is a student at a film school in Los Angeles. ( )
2. All the students in the film school are looking for work in the film industry.

   ( )
3. Many studios in the film industry are willing to employ women. ( )
4. There have been many woman directors who are successful. ( )
5. Many female directors were nominated for Oscars recently. ( )

31

3 | Listening Practice 2

WEB動画 | DVD | CD | 1-19

Listen to the recording and fill in the missing words.

Narrator : Here at this Los Angeles film school, Liz is in charge of changing the sets between takes. She will graduate in three months time and hopes to join the next generation of women in Hollywood.

in charge of ～の担当

between takes
1回分の撮影 (場面) の間

Liz Holland: They tell us all the same thing, be true to your vision, be true to yourself, and don't be bullied.
¹(   ) (   )
(   ) (   )
(   ) boys and men who respect women, and who respect female DPs, and who respect female directors.

DP 撮影監督

Narrator : 90 percent of the students on this set are women. But all the students know that they will be looking for work in a film industry that has been turned upside down by numerous sexual assault scandals and the #MeToo and #TimesUp movements.

#MeToo 性的嫌がらせなどの被害体験を告白・共有する際に使用されるSNSのハッシュタグ
#TimesUp 職場でのハラスメントを受けた人に法的な補助を提供する基金のハッシュタグ

Quran Squire: Would I want this to happen to me or to someone that I know? No. So
²(   ) (   )
(   ) (   )
(   ) the next person, and again just be the ally, be there, be the voice, be the ears, and be the movement when I need to be that.

Narrator : One of the greatest hurdles facing women in the industry is that many studios are still hesitant to put them at the helm of major blockbusters. Of the 10 biggest box office successes of 2017, only one film, *Wonder Woman,* ³(   ) (   )
(   ) (   ) (   ).

at the helm
～の指導的立場にある
blockbuster 大ヒット作
Wonder Woman
アメリカ映画 (2017年)

Marlee Roberts: Hiring women and putting them in leadership positions, putting them as the lead in a role, giving them substantial roles that have weight and have depth, I think we need to prove to the studios and to the industry, and I think we have proven, that those are not risks anymore. I think that was evident by last year's success in *Wonder Woman*.

Narrator: To build on the success of *Wonder Woman*, Warner Brothers has created a program ⁴( ) ( ) ( ) ( ) in filmmaking. The fund helped Carla embark on a $160,000 scriptwriter's degree.

scriptwriter 脚本家

Carla Arellano: I'm trying to create something new, I'm kind of sick of seeing billboards on buses of the same white actors selling the same white stories… How many more white families on television do we need to see?

billboard 広告板

Narrator : Despite recent box office successes from the likes of *Lady Bird*, ⁵( ) ( ) ( ) ( ) ( ) an Oscar, and the nearly all black cast of *Black Panther*, diversity both in front of and behind the camera remains the exception, not the norm.

box office success 大当たり
Lady Bird アメリカ映画 (2017年)
Oscar アカデミー賞
Black Panther アメリカ映画 (2018年)

---

4 | Comprehension Check | *Second Viewing*

WEB動画 🖥 DVD

Watch the news clip again and answer the following questions in English.

1. When will Liz Holland graduate from the film school?

....

2. What percent of the students on the set are women?

....

3. What has turned the film industry in Los Angeles upside down?

....

4. What is one of the greatest hurdles facing women in the film industry?

....

5. What does Marlee Roberts think women need to prove?

....

Listen to the recording and complete the summary.

The entertainment industry is taking a long, hard look at itself, following a tidal ¹( ) of sexual assault claims against film directors and producers. Hollywood's next generation seeks to be the ²( ) for change. Despite the recent successes of *Lady Bird* and *Black Panther*, diversity both in front of and behind the camera remains the ³( ).

❚❚ READING

1-21

In 2018, the world economic report placed Japan 110th out of 144 countries in gender equality. This was four places higher than the year before, but still a long way from the top.
5 Differences in education, income, and workplace power reflect many of the inequalities that still exist worldwide. The report is clear that much needs to
10 be done to change the situation.

Gender equality means that both men and women are given the same chance to reach their goals in all areas of life. Women, however, are more often denied fair treatment and the same chances as men. They are not given the option to make choices that impact their personal lives or the places they live. Being equal means women can
15 receive a good education, can be a part of the workforce, and can develop their skills. It also means that they share the role of raising children, and do not face violence in the workplace or at home. In developing countries, harmful cultural and social practices frequently feature in international news stories. Issues such as marriage and reproductive health rights have highlighted the inequalities and biases of many
20 systems. These have a major influence on how much women can earn, their work opportunities, and the safety of their children and families. Developed countries also face scrutiny. The #MeToo campaign has focused on the violence and threats that women face in almost every walk of life.

Gender parity has increased in recent years. The slow progress, however, is clearly a concern as are the large gender gaps that continue to divide men and women.

(266 words)

Notes

parity 等価、同等

1 Vocabulary Check

Fill in the blanks with the most appropriate words from the list below.

1. There has been a (   ) that microplastics pollute water.
2. The proposal was (   ) by the committee.
3. You should not leave (   ) belongings unattended.
4. Kangaroos only (   ) in Australia.
5. The financial report is under (   ) by a third-party now.

> exist   denied   personal   scrutiny   concern

2 Comprehension Questions

Answer the following questions in English.

1. In which place did Japan rank in the world economic report on gender equality in 2018?

   ....

2. Was the result higher or lower compared to 2017?

   ....

3. What does gender equality mean?

   ....

4. What issues have highlighted the inequalities in developing countries?

   ....

5. What has the #MeToo campaign focused on?

   ....

3 Grammar Check

Unscramble the following words and complete the sentences.

1. The population of Tokyo is [New York, of, larger, that, than].
   The population of Tokyo is ....
2. Zoe [to, electric, able, the, is, guitar, play] very well.
   Zoe .... very well.
3. Getting enough sleep [influence, a, positive, has, on] our health.
   Getting enough sleep .... our health.

 **DISCUSSION**

Goal 5: GENDER EQUALITY
Why it matters

上級管理職や中間管理職に就いている女性は、平均して3人に1人以下です。 そのため、以下の目標が挙げられています。

Goal	To achieve gender equality and empower all women and girls. (男女平等を達成し、すべての女性と女子に権限を与える)

この目標を達成するために、私たちに何ができるでしょうか？ 以下に挙げる例から自分ができると思う行動を1つ選び、その理由をクラスで発表しましょう。

Daily actions you may want to take:

1. Practice and demonstrate to children equal decision-making processes at home.
2. Encourage schools to provide scholarships for girls.
3. If you are a woman, know your rights and stand up for them.
4. Make flexibility and work-life balance a part of the company's culture.
5. Make gender equality part of training and education. Young people should be supported in choosing jobs that advance their future, regardless of their gender.
6. Gender equality starts at home.

番号： _____

理由	
具体的な行動	

Clean Water & Sanitation

Avoid wasting water

　世界では、10 人のうち 3 人が安全な飲料水が入手できていないといわれています。安全な飲み水ときれいなトイレの衛生は、人権問題です。すべての人が安全な飲料水ときれいなトイレを利用可能にするために、あなたは何ができますか。

❶ LISTENING

1 | Key Word Study | *Before Watching the Video*

Match each word with its definition.

1. brunt   (   )   2. cultivar   (   )   3. estimate   (   )
4. negative   (   )   5. prompt   (   )   6. renowned   (   )
7. restriction (   )   8. shortfall   (   )   9. slump   (   )
10. sustain   (   )

a. 不足	b. 有名な	c. 耐える	d. 駆り立てる	e. 制限
f. 否定的な	g. 大きな負担	h. 栽培品種	i. がた落ちする	j. 推定

2 | Listening Practice 1 | *First Viewing*   (Time 01:59) 📺 💿 DVD

Watch the news clip and write T if the statement is true or F if it is false.

1. There has been severe drought for three years in the Western Cape.   (   )
2. The drought causes the berries to become larger.   (   )
3. Winemakers are considering vines that can sustain the heat and drought.

　　　　　　　　　　　　　　　　　　　　　　　　　　　　　　　　　　　　(   )
4. Fruit growers feel that they need to cut down labor costs.   (   )
5. Day Zero is estimated to come next month.   (   )

WEB動画 DVD CD 1-23

Listen to the recording and fill in the missing words.

Narrator: A three-year-long drought in the Western Cape has caused the region's dams to reach critically low water levels, prompting the government to declare a national disaster. Individuals are being limited to just 50 liters a day to prevent a shut-off. Water restrictions have not just hit families, but businesses too, including the region's world-renowned wine industry.

Western Cape
南アフリカ共和国南西部の州

Marlize Jacobs: Well, the berries are smaller to start with because [1](   ) (   ) (   ) (   ) and it really actually improves the quality to a certain extent, but it's not very sustainable to farm like that because the smaller your berry the less is your yield. So you have a smaller harvest and obviously when you have a smaller harvest you have less wine to sell at the end of the day. So it's a financial impact.

to a certain extent
ある程度まで

Narrator: [2](   ) (   ) (   ) (   ) by about 20 percent over the last 12 months, forcing winemakers like Marlize to consider vines that require less water.

vine ブドウ

Marlize Jacobs: Obviously we're looking into getting grape cultivars that can sustain the heat and the drought. Spanish cultivars are very popular, as well as Italian cultivars that doesn't need as much water. So I think there will be a general shift but it's very difficult [3](   ) (   ) (   ) (   ) (   ) (   ) or recognize those wines.

Narrator: Fruit growers are also feeling the brunt with industry bodies warning that thousands of jobs are on the line.

on the line 危険にさらされて

Jacques Du Preez: In a situation like this there's a very big focus on ⁴(   ) (   ) (   ) (   ). Because you don't know what next year will hold for you, so there will be a negative impact on labor usage.

Narrator: It seems the efforts have paid off, with the estimate for the so-called Day Zero, when taps run dry, pushed back from next month, to 2019. In the meantime, South Africa's wine industry can ⁵(   ) (   ) (   ) (   ) (   ) to make up the shortfall.

Day Zero ケープタウンの街の水道が遮断される日

---

4 | Comprehension Check | *Second Viewing*

WEB動画 🖥️ **DVD**

Watch the news clip again and answer the following questions in English.

1. How many liters are individuals limited to use per day to prevent a shut-off of water?

    ....

2. By what percentage has wine production decreased over the last 12 months?

    ....

3. What kinds of grape cultivars can sustain the heat and the drought?

    ....

4. What negative impact does the drought have?

    ....

5. When was Day Zero estimated to happen?

    ....

5 | Summary

Listen to the recording and complete the summary.

The Western Cape region has gone without significant rains for more than three years, forcing South Africa's second city to slash water ¹(   ) by more than 60 percent. The city was granted a narrow ²(   ) earlier this month when the dreaded "Day Zero" — the date when taps will run dry — was finally ³(   ) back until next year after months of growing public panic.

▮▮ READING

1-25

Water is the most important resource for sustaining human life. Demand around the world for this resource is growing. And yet, with the problems of climate change and
5 pollution billions of people face a lack of access to clean, sanitary water.

Member states of the United Nations all agree that it is a human right to have access to water and sanitation. Water is vital for all
10 forms of food security, health, and economic welfare. However, of the targets set by the UN, fewer than half of the member states have collected data to monitor progress. Moreover, only six percent have supplied data on more than eight of the 17 sustainable development goals. Very few countries will be able to offer universal basic water services before 2030. Without action close to a billion people will lack clean drinking
15 water and another 2.1 billion will lack sources of water for homes, schools, or other public places. This is a concern, as without fresh water, people are unable to wash their hands regularly, a major cause of disease transmission.

The largest user of water is agriculture. 69 percent of all the water consumed each year is pumped from the ground to use on farms. Only 12 percent is used by
20 households. The problem is that most waste water from agricultural sources is put back into water systems without being treated. This further reduces the fresh water available and causes more damage to the ecosystem.

Supplying fresh water to all those that need it is therefore a major priority. It will need strong leadership to make better use of available resources and protect ecosystems through recycling and sustainable approaches.   (276 words)

Notes
....
sanitary 清潔な   **ecosystem** 生態系

40

1 Vocabulary Check

Fill in the blanks with the most appropriate words from the list below.

1. Retail shops need to carefully analyze the (   ) for the items they sell.

2. Teachers (   ) activities by walking around the room.

3. The committee decided to (   ) the position to Rachel.

4. Natural gas is a (   ) found in many parts of the world.

5. Recycling has made it possible to (   ) the amount of waste.

> resource   demand   monitor   offer   reduce

2 Comprehension Questions

Answer the following questions in English.

1. What do member states of the United Nations all agree?

   ....

2. Why is water important?

   ....

3. How many people will lack clean drinking water without action?

   ....

4. What sector is the largest user of water?

   ....

5. What is the problem of waste water from agricultural sources?

   ....

3 Grammar Check

Unscramble the following words and complete the sentences.

1. [seminar, the, half, members, of] are going to attend the conference.

   .... are going to attend the conference.

2. Fully self-driving cars [become, 2025, available, may, before].

   Fully self-driving cars ....

3. Students asked the teacher to turn off the heater [too, it, getting, was, warm, as].

   Students asked the teacher to turn off the heater ....

 **DISCUSSION**

Goal 6: CLEAN WATER AND SANITATION
Why it matters

10人に3人が、安全に管理された飲料水の提供を受けられていません。そのような状況を避けるため、以下の目標が挙げられています。

Goal	To ensure access to safe water sources and sanitation for all. （安全な飲料水を入手することと衛生をすべての人に確保する）

この目標を達成するために、私たちに何ができるでしょうか？　以下に挙げる例から自分ができると思う行動を1つ選び、その理由をクラスで発表しましょう。

Daily actions you may want to take:

1. Read a book on water. It will increase your understanding of the impact water has on societies, economies, and our planet.

2. Conserve, conserve, conserve. When ice-cubes are left over from a drink, don't throw them away. Put them into plants.

3. Support organizations that give water to areas in need.

4. Donate to projects that require funds for digging boreholes, installing pipes and pumps, maintenance training to communities, etc.

5. Never flush toxic chemicals such as paints, chemicals, or medication down the toilet. It pollutes lakes and rivers and causes health problems in marine life and humans.

6. Turn off the tap when brushing your teeth and while soaping in the shower.

番号：＿＿＿＿＿＿

理由	
具体的な行動	

Affordable & Clean Energy

Use only energy efficient appliances and light bulbs

世界中のすべての人が、エネルギー効率の良い電球に切り替えると、年間 1200 億円が節約できるといわれています。すべての人にクリーンなエネルギーを提供するために、あなたは何ができますか。

I LISTENING

1 | Key Word Study | *Before Watching the Video*

Match each word with its definition.

1. acquire ( )   2. bandit ( )   3. blacken ( )

4. cough ( )   5. dazzling ( )   6. equipped with ( )

7. isolated ( )   8. nostril ( )   9. properly ( )

10. scared ( )

a. 習得する	b. 〜を装備した	c. 鼻の穴	d. 正確に	e. 盗賊
f. 孤立した	g. 咳をする	h. 黒くする	i. 怖がって	j. まぶしい

2 | Listening Practice 1 | *First Viewing* (Time 01:59) WEB動画 DVD

Watch the news clip and write T if the statement is true or F if it is false.

1. The village in western Madagascar uses only oil lamps. ( )

2. The smoke from the lamps causes children to cough. ( )

3. Four Indian women learned the skill of installing the equipment. ( )

4. Solar energy helps increase security in the village. ( )

5. Ninety-four percent of the people in the village have electricity. ( )

Listen to the recording and fill in the missing words.

Narrator: Up until the end of 2017, this isolated fishing village in western Madagascar had no access to electricity; Yollande and her grandchildren used oil lamps as their light source.

Madagascar マダガスカル

Yollande Randrianambinina: First, there wasn't enough light, ¹(   ) (   ) (   ) (   ). And then, the smoke made us sick. The children did not stop coughing, and they had blackened nostrils.

Narrator: Today nearly 200 homes are equipped with solar panels, and it is Yollande and three other women from the village who install and repair the equipment, a skill acquired in India, where ²(   ) (   ) (   ) (   ) (   ) (   ).

Kingeline: When we left, I was a little scared because we didn't know this country. ³(   ) (   ) (   ) (   ) were the lights!

Ahh, it was really dazzling to see all those lights in India. We had lights on all the time, non-stop. The fan ran all day long, as did the electricity. There was no power failure.

Narrator: The program has changed the lives of the villagers, who can now continue to study, work, or cook in the evenings. Solar energy can also help increase security.

Yollande Randrianambinina: There have already been two deaths here, they were shot dead. That's why we wanted ⁴(   ) (   ) (   )

(   ) to see the bandits from afar, and be able to escape in time or prepare.

from afar 遠くから

Narrator: By 2030, the project plans to supply 630,000 households with solar energy. [5](   ) (   ) (   ) for a country where 94 percent of the population is still without electricity.

---

4 | Comprehension Check | *Second Viewing*

WEB動画 DVD

Watch the news clip again and answer the following questions in English.

1. When did this village gain access to electricity?

   ....

2. What were the problems of oil lamps?

   ....

3. How many homes are now equipped with solar panels?

   ....

4. How did Kingeline feel when she left the village for India?

   ....

5. What does the project plan to do by 2030?

   ....

5 | Summary

1-28

Listen to the recording and complete the summary.

In March 2016, thanks to a [1](   ) between the NGO World Wildlife Fund and Barefoot College, four women from the remote village in the West of Madagascar [2](   ) for India to become "solar technicians." Back in their village after 6 months of training, they are now able to install, repair, and [3](   ) the photovoltaic panels.

Without energy, none of the United Nation's goals would be achieved. Energy is vital to programs that reduce poverty, secure food supplies, and protect public health. Clean energy will one day play a major role in providing constant, cheap fuel to over three billion people in need. Currently, however, it has not been able to meet
5 the demands of a growing population. Since 2014, fewer people have access to either electricity or clean fuel.

A reliable supply of energy is particularly challenging for those in rural areas. The landscape and level of use restrict its distribution. A constant supply is needed to allow productive activities, lighting in homes, or hospitals to tend patients 24
10 hours a day. A practical example of a new affordable energy is cooking fuel. This uses compressed natural gas, petroleum gas, or a blend called gasohol. Clean fuels are safer, better for health, and do less damage to the environment than fossil fuels. In 2017, however, 38 percent of the world's population lacked access to clean cooking. They continue to cook with inefficient stoves or over open fires.

15 The problem with energy supply is the cost. Areas without it are often in the poorest regions. These communities lack the resources and infrastructure to establish a power grid. Off-grid local systems and solar panels, however, are becoming cheaper and more effective. To widen access new ways must be found to inform, educate, and supply users.

20 It is hoped clean energy costs will continue to fall and become more efficient. This will allow more of the world's population to gain access to the benefits of continuous and secure energy. (271 words)

Notes
....
compressed 圧縮した

1 | Vocabulary Check

Fill in the blanks with the most appropriate words from the list below.

1. The price of (   ) affects the price of plane tickets.

2. We had a (   ) meeting and reached an agreement.

3. James has been driving at a (   ) speed for two hours.

4. Different (   ) of Japan have different local food.

5. Some large cities lack (   ) housing.

regions	fuel	constant	productive	affordable

2 | Comprehension Questions

Answer the following questions in English.

1. To what programs is energy vital?

   ....

2. Why is a constant supply of energy needed?

   ....

3. Why are clean fuels better than fossil fuels?

   ....

4. What is the problem with energy supply?

   ....

5. What are becoming cheaper and more effective?

   ....

3 | Grammar Check

Unscramble the following words and complete the sentences.

1. [Japan, playing, been, important, an, role, has] in dealing with environmental problems.

   .... in dealing with environmental problems.

2. The next meeting [Tuesday, be, either, or, on, will, held] Wednesday.

   The next meeting .... Wednesday.

3. Polar bears are an [endangered, of, example, species, an].

   Polar bears are an ....

Goal 7: AFFORDABLE AND CLEAN ENERGY
Why it matters

世界中の人々がエネルギー効率の高い電球に切り替えた場合、世界は年間 1,200 億ドル節約できます。 そのため、以下の目標が挙げられています。

Goal	To ensure access to affordable, reliable, sustainable, and modern energy for all. （手頃な価格で、信頼でき、持続可能で、そして現代的なエネルギーへのアクセスをすべての人に確保する）

この目標を達成するために、私たちに何ができるでしょうか？ 以下に挙げる例から自分ができると思う行動を 1 つ選び、その理由をクラスで発表しましょう。

Daily actions you may want to take:

1. Cover pans with a lid. It reduces the amount of energy required to boil water by 75 percent.
2. Turn off electronic equipment such as TVs and computers when going on holiday.
3. Turn lights off in rooms that aren't being used. When you switch your lights off, even for a few seconds, it saves more energy than it takes for the light to start up, regardless of the bulb type.
4. Use energy-efficient lightbulbs and put your household appliances on low-energy settings.
5. Support solar power projects for schools, homes, and offices.
6. Only fill the kettle with the amount of water needed.

番号：_____

理由	
具体的な行動	

48

Buy from green companies

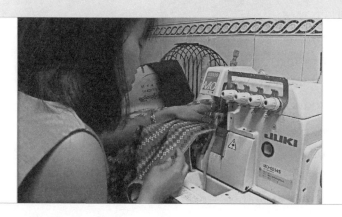

世界の労働者人口に仕事を供給するためには、毎年 3000 万件の新たな雇用が必要です。22 億人が 1 日当たり 1.90 ドル以下で暮らしています。働きがいと経済成長を成し遂げるために、あなたは何ができますか。

I LISTENING

1 Key Word Study | *Before Watching the Video*

Match each word with its definition.

1. churn out ( )   2. conscience ( )   3. consequence ( )

4. couture ( )   5. determine ( )   6. disrupt ( )

7. pile into ( )   8. toil ( )   9. unethical ( )

10. weaving industry ( )

a. 骨折って働く	b. 大量生産する	c. 混乱させる	d. 非倫理的な
e. 高級婦人服仕立て	f. 決心する g. 織物業	h. 結果 i. 良心 j. 押しかける	

2 Listening Practice 1 | *First Viewing*   (Time 01:55) WEB動画 📺 DVD

Watch the news clip and write T if the statement is true or F if it is false.

1. Pyone Thet Thet Kyaw is a clothing factory worker.   ( )

2. Global brands have been banned in Myanmar since 2011.   ( )

3. The traditional weaving industry in Myanmar has been dying.   ( )

4. Aung San Suu Kyi famously wears traditional Myanmar clothing.   ( )

5. Workers in clothing factories can spend 10 minutes to go to the toilet.   ( )

WEB動画 DVD CD 1-31

Listen to the recording and fill in the missing words.

Narrator: Made in Myanmar — with a conscience. This designer once toiled as a teenage worker in a factory outside Yangon churning out clothes. Now she is one of a new crop of designers using homegrown couture as a counter to cheap, mass-produced fashion.

as a counter to
〜と正反対として

Pyone Thet Thet Kyaw: We are the one dealing with the consequences of the situation, [1]( ) ( ) ( ). So if this fast fashion and the unethical fashion continues, then we're the ones to be suffering.

Narrator: Global brands like H&M and Primark have piled into Myanmar since junta rule ended in 2011. Garment exports more than doubled to $1.65 billion last year. But critics say low wages, long hours and weak labor rights mean [2]( ) ( ) ( ) ( ). Others fear the flood of low-cost clothes is killing off a centuries-old traditional weaving industry.

H&M スウェーデンのファストファッションの会社
Primark アイルランドのファストファッションの会社
junta rule 軍事政権による支配

Mo Hom: The local mills are actually dying because there is no market demand anymore. [3]( ) ( ) ( ) ( ) ( ), so they don't have buyers as much as they're supposed to have, so a lot of the mills are actually closing down.

Narrator: Myanmar is proud of its traditional clothing — [4]( ) ( ) ( ) ( ) ( ) Aung San Suu Kyi. Today there are some 50 designers compared to just 10 in 1994. Pyone Thet Thet Kyaw's experience on the

Aung San Suu Kyi
アウン・サン・スー・チー

factory floor made her determined to open her own boutique and train other women.

Pyone Thet Thet Kyaw: I started to see some of the things, like you only get to spend like 10 minutes of your time for lunch and you cannot go to the toilet ⁵( ) ( ) ( ) because it would disrupt the production line.

Narrator: Aiming to make sure workers — and local fabrics – don't get left behind. Stitch by stitch.

get left behind 取り残される
stitch by stitch 一針ずつ

---

4 | Comprehension Check | *Second Viewing*

WEB動画 🖥 💿 DVD

Watch the news clip again and answer the following questions in English.

1. What did Pyone Thet Thet Kyaw do as a teenager?

    ....

2. What have become popular after 2011 in Myanmar?

    ....

3. How did garment exports change last year?

    ....

4. What has happened to the number of designers of traditional clothing since 1994?

    ....

5. What problems do the workers in clothing factories face?

    ....

5 | Summary

💿 1-32

Listen to the recording and complete the summary.

With Myanmar emerging as a manufacturing hub for mass-produced clothes, a crop of young ¹( ) are using home-grown fashion to preserve the country's sartorial heritage and reshape the ²( ) model. A recent report by multinational watchdog SOMO warned of "significant risks of labor rights violations being committed in Myanmar's garment industry that need to be addressed as a matter of ³( )".

Statistics show that good progress has been made toward increasing the global number of productive, high-quality jobs.
5 However, many countries do not have the conditions to promote decent work for all. Many workers must find informal employment that is not counted
10 in statistics.

Not having all the figures makes it difficult to know the true state of a labor market. Having no information has a negative impact on working and living conditions for the workers. It also has an impact on the country itself as productivity is reduced and salaries remain low.
15 In these circumstances, it is difficult to find information on the people who are excluded from decent employment. This may be because of age, race, or disability. In many countries, it is women who are more likely to be working in part-time or low-level jobs. Positions in agriculture or factories often employ high numbers of female workers. These sectors are often low paid with poor working conditions.

20 Job statistics are usually collected to show whether a person is either in or out of work. This measure, however, is insufficient. To earn money, unemployed people often take any job available. These jobs may be short-term, unstable, or outside the system. In such cases, it is difficult to know how many hours a person works or how much they earn. Although in work, they may be barely surviving above the poverty
25 line. The work may also be seasonal or far from their homes or family.

The United Nations aims to help create the conditions for good work opportunities. It believes that education, training, and support will lead to inclusive practices, end poverty, and provide decent jobs for all.

(278 words)

Notes
inclusive 包括的な

1 Vocabulary Check

Fill in the blanks with the most appropriate words from the list below.

1. We have made good (   ) on the project.
2. The outcome of the initiative (   ) uncertain.
3. Some age groups are (   ) from the data.
4. (   ) show that there are more cats than dogs in Japanese households.
5. Ground can become (   ) after heavy rain.

statistics   progress   unstable   remains   excluded

2 Comprehension Questions

Answer the following questions in English.

1. What good progress has been made according to statistics?

   ....

2. What do many workers have to find in reality?

   ....

3. What job sectors have high numbers of female workers?

   ....

4. What are job statistics usually based on?

   ....

5. Why is this measure insufficient?

   ....

3 Grammar Check

Unscramble the following words and complete the sentences.

1. [data, enough, having, can, not] result in wrong conclusions.

   .... result in wrong conclusions.

2. New Zealand is a popular tourist destination [of, its, nature, because, beautiful].

   New Zealand is a popular tourist destination ....

3. Effective promotion [to, in, an, increase, leads, customers].

   Effective promotion ....

Goal 8: DECENT WORK AND ECONOMIC GROWTH
Why it matters

3,000万人：世界の労働年齢人口の増加に追いつくために、労働市場への新規参入に毎年必要な仕事の数です。 そのため、以下の目標が挙げられています。

Goal	To promote inclusive and sustainable economic growth, employment and decent work for all. （包括的かつ持続可能な経済成長、雇用、きちんとした仕事をすべての人に促進する）

この目標を達成するために、私たちに何ができるでしょうか？　以下に挙げる例から自分ができると思う行動を１つ選び、その理由をクラスで発表しましょう。

Daily actions you may want to take:

1. Encourage Bring Your Child to Work Day so that young people can see what a healthy work environment looks like.
2. Support international campaigns to end modern-day slavery, forced labor, human trafficking, and forced marriages.
3. Provide food for low-earning workers.
4. Provide incentives for hard work. People respond to a reward system.
5. Ensure safe working conditions.
6. Encourage more job opportunities for young people.

番号：＿＿＿＿＿

理由	
具体的な行動	

Think of innovative new ways to repurpose old material

　経済成長と社会の発展は、インフラ整備や持続可能な産業の発展や技術革新に大いに依存しています。製造業の1件の雇用は、ほかの分野での2.2件の雇用を生み出すといわれています。産業と技術革新の基盤を築くためにあなたは何ができますか。

① LISTENING

1 | Key Word Study | *Before Watching the Video*

Match each word with its definition.

1. bit　　　　　　(　　)　　2. contemporary　　(　　)　　3. core　　　　　　(　　)

4. deconstruct　(　　)　　5. garment　　　　　(　　)　　6. incredible　　(　　)

7. ingredient　(　　)　　8. manufacture　　(　　)　　9. rim　　　　　　(　　)

10. source　　　(　　)

a. 材料	b. 信じられないほど素晴らしい	c. 一片	d. 製作する
e. 分解する	f. 衣類　g. 現代の　h. 調達する	i. 縁	j. 中心的な

2 | Listening Practice 1 | *First Viewing*　　　　　(Time 01:50) 🖥️ 💿DVD

Watch the news clip and write T if the statement is true or F if it is false.

1. Christopher Raeburn remakes, reduces, and recycles old garments.　　(　　)

2. He works in a studio in East London.　　(　　)

3. He recycled parachutes and made blankets.　　(　　)

4. He makes small bags from 70-year-old silk maps.　　(　　)

5. He thinks remaking garments is a big industry.　　(　　)

Listen to the recording and fill in the missing words.

Christopher Raeburn: My name's Christopher Raeburn. We're here actually in the Remade Studio in East London. So as a business we only do three things–we either  remake, reduce, or recycle, and what that really means with "Remade" is ¹( ) ( ) ( ) ( ), and we've worked over the years with everything from beautiful parachutes to life-rafts to blankets, you name it we've taken it apart and made it into something useful again.

parachutes パラシュート
life-rafts 救命ボート

Katherine George: So this used to be a compression flight suit used by Chinese fighter pilots, and we're basically ²( )  ( ) ( ) ( ) ( ) to make these small bags. And we take different bits, like off the edge where the tubing goes, and that makes the rim that runs around the edge here, and then we get all the cool details.

compression flight suit
圧縮型飛行用スーツ

off the edge ～の縁[端]

tubing 縁取り

Christopher Raeburn: We make garments for both men and women from original 1950s silk maps, and ³( ) ( ) ( ), they were made for the Royal Air Force and they used to print onto silk which has incredible quality, so again this isn't a new fabric, it's actually 70-year-old silk that we've been able to source and then completely remake into the garments you see here. The real skill and I'd like to think the value that we bring actually is around the fact that we're completely deconstructing those original items, we're looking

Royal Air Force 英国空軍

at those core ingredients and then [4](   )
(   ) (   ) (   )
(   ) (   ) completely new, something contemporary, something wearable. The guardsmen's jackets that you might see at Buckingham Palace, completely deconstructed. What's fantastic is that I do think the industry's changing, [5](   ) (   ) (   ) (   ) (   ) around the way that we're sourcing materials, manufacturing, all of those things, but it takes time, it's a very, very, very big industry. And I think if we can all work together then we've got a much better chance of really making a difference.

guardsmen's jackets
近衛兵の上着
Buckingham Palace
バッキンガム宮殿

---

4 | Comprehension Check | *Second Viewing*

WEB動画   DVD

Watch the news clip again and answer the following questions in English.

1. Who used compression flight suits?

    ....

2. What was the compression flight suit made into?

    ....

3. Who were the silk maps made for?

    ....

4. Where might we see the guardsman's jackets?

    ....

5. What does Raeburn think is fantastic?

    ....

5 | Summary

CD 2-03

Listen to the recording and complete the summary.

Environmental awareness isn't something you'd always [1](   ) with high fashion, but designer Christopher Raeburn is changing that perception. Everything he makes is "reduced, reused, or ²(   )," with old silk maps and Chinese fighter pilots' flight suits just some of the discarded materials he ³(   ) into new creations.

⏸ READING

2-04

Clearly, the growth of developing countries should be guided by a sustainable approach. As economies grow, they must think about the
5 welfare of future generations. History has shown that great harm can be done by polluting the environment or depleting resources. In the long term, sustainability will create the
10 conditions to provide higher quality goods and services. This will improve the lives of workers by creating more stable jobs and bring countries closer to ending poverty.

To grow an economy, a basic infrastructure is vital. It provides the basic needs for businesses and society. The cost of structure is high, but is key to growth. It includes
15 roads, communications, and water and electric systems. Investing in new systems can provide construction jobs, improve productivity, and give more access to markets. Many countries, however, lack this basic structure.

Infrastructure allows countries to industrialize. Many developing nations are able to find cheap labor and natural resources. To develop, however, entails adapting to
20 new, cleaner technology. This allows them to compete in the markets. The United Nations is helping to finance new technology in small businesses. It hopes this will promote the growth of jobs in these and other sectors.

As they industrialize, developing countries must innovate. There is a need to find alternative solutions to problems in industries such as farming or energy. As
25 countries develop, competition between companies will demand technologies that meet the needs of local people and businesses.

Sustainable development is key to economic growth. The problem will be in finding a balance between economic, environmental, and social goals.   (260 words)

Notes
entail 〜を必然的に伴う

58

1 Vocabulary Check

Fill in the blanks with the most appropriate words from the list below.

1. Wastewater from factories can (   ) rivers.

2. Some natural resources are likely to be (   ) in the near future.

3. Finland is known for its comprehensive (   ).

4. The invention of machinery (   ) England rapidly in the 18th century.

5. It is important to carefully consider how to (   ) money.

depleted   pollute   invest   industrialized   welfare

2 Comprehension Questions

Answer the following questions in English.

1. What will sustainability create in the long term?

   ....

2. What is vital to grow an economy?

   ....

3. What does a basic infrastructure include?

   ....

4. What is the United Nations helping to finance?

   ....

5. What do developing countries need to find for problems in industries?

   ....

3 Grammar Check

Unscramble the following words and complete the sentences.

1. Some large cities are [trying, become, city, cleaner, to, a].

   Some large cities are ....

2. Animals have evolved [to, by, environment, a, adapting, new].

   Animals have evolved ....

3. There has been intense competition [the, two, companies, leading, computer, between].

   There has been intense competition ....

   ....

 **DISCUSSION**

Goal 9: INDUSTRY, INNOVATION AND INFRASTRUCTURE
Why it matters

工業化の雇用拡大効果は、社会に良い影響を与えます。 製造業における一つの仕事は他の部門において 2.2 の雇用を生み出します。 そのため、以下の目標が挙げられています。

Goal	To build resilient infrastructure, promote inclusive and sustainable industrialization, and foster innovation. （柔軟性のあるインフラを構築し、包括的かつ持続可能な産業化を促進し、革新を促進する）

この目標を達成するために、私たちに何ができるでしょうか？ 以下に挙げる例から自分ができると思う行動を１つ選び、その理由をクラスで発表しましょう。

Daily actions you may want to take:

1. Fund projects that provide infrastructure for basic needs.

2. Encourage sustainable infrastructure with efficient resources and environmentally friendly technologies.

3. Keep up to date with the latest technologies and innovation.

4. Invest in domestic technology development research and innovation in developing countries.

5. Make cities healthy. Turn empty roof space on buildings into green roofs. They improve air quality, insulation by up to 25 percent, they absorb sound, promote social integration, and more.

6. Don't throw away, give away. Upgrading our electronic gadgets is inevitable, but often our gadgets are still in good working condition. Pass on your old working devices or recycle them as certain parts can be recovered.

番号：＿＿＿＿＿

理由	
具体的な行動	

Raise your voice against discrimination

世界のいかなる人々も除外すると、持続可能な開発目標は達成できません。収入、性別、年齢、障がい、人種、宗教などによる差別は、長期的な社会や経済の発展を阻害しています。人や国の不平等をなくすために、あなたは何ができますか。

I LISTENING

I | Key Word Study | *Before Watching the Video*

Match each word with its definition.

1. acknowledge ( )   2. criminalize ( )   3. dominate ( )

4. explode ( )   5. milestone ( )   6. permission ( )

7. protester ( )   8. rebel ( )   9. restrictive ( )

10. tolerance ( )

| a. 爆発的に増える | b. 支配する | c. 制限しようとする | d. 認める | e. 反逆者 |
| f. 容認 | g. 許可 | h. 違法とする | i. 画期的出来事 | j. 抗議をする人 |

2 | Listening Practice 1 | *First Viewing*   (Time 02:07) 📱 💿 DVD

Watch the news clip and write T if the statement is true or F if it is false.

1. The LGBT festival has been held in public many times in Myanmar. ( )

2. This event was held in a stadium in Yangon. ( )

3. Hla Myat Tun thinks the event is for acknowledging equality and basic human rights. ( )

4. Aung Myo Min spent some years in the jungle as an armed rebel against military rule. ( )

5. Activists hope to get rid of the law criminalizing the LGBT community. ( )

Listen to the recording and fill in the missing words.

Narrator : From handbag-throwing and racing in heels to showing off your prowess with a hula hoop… or not. Myanmar's drag queen olympics are just one of the  highlights of the country's biggest ever LGBT festival, taking place in a public park for the first time. A milestone for the community in a country where same-sex relations are still officially illegal.

prowess 優れた能力
hula hoop フラフープ
drag queen
女装の男性同性愛者

LGBT 性的少数者

same-sex relations 同性愛

Thaw Zin: Some people don't know about LGBT people. You get people who are LGBT but ¹( )
( ) ( )
( ) ( )
( ). They don't understand. So that's why it's difficult for other people to understand as well.

Narrator : Organizers were happily surprised to be granted permission to hold the event in the park in downtown Yangon. ²( ) ( )
( ) ( ) means that numbers have exploded with some 6,000 people turning up on the first day alone.

be granted 認められる

Hla Myat Tun: So I would say this is not just for the LGBT community. This is for the whole country, acknowledging equality and basic human rights.

Narrator : LGBT-focused documentaries ³( )
( ) ( ) ( )
throughout the two-weekend event. The film *This Kind of Love* charts activist Aung Myo Min's life from student protester in 1988 to the years he spent in the jungle as an armed rebel against military rule. He hopes he can help break down stereotypes.

This Kind of Love
ミャンマーのドキュメンタリー映画(2015)
Aung Myo Min ミャンマーの平等事務局長

stereotype 固定概念

Aung Myo Min: People were really surprised to see gay men

like me on stage, ⁴(   ) (   )
(   ) (   ) and I went to the
jungle, which is totally dominated by macho men and | **macho men** 男っぽい男
very restrictive military rules. So I survived.

Narrator : As tolerance increases, activists now hope the next
step will be getting rid of the law criminalizing | **get rid of** ～を一掃する
the community. The festival will take to the road
later this year ⁵(   )
(   ) (   )
(   ) (   )
— and the partying — across the
country.

---

4 | Comprehension Check | *Second Viewing* 　WEB動画 🖥 🎞 DVD

Watch the news clip again and answer the following questions in English.

1. How are same-sex relations regarded in Myanmar?

   ....

2. How did organizers feel when receiving permission to hold the event?

   ....

3. How many people turned up on the first day?

   ....

4. What does the movie *This Kind of Love* describe?

   ....

5. How did people react to seeing gay men on stage?

   ....

5 | Summary 　🎧 2-07

Listen to the recording and complete the summary.

Fluorescent wigs askew and leaving broken stiletto heels and a cloud of glitter in
their wake, Myanmar drag queens ¹(   ) across the finish line and crashed
into a waiting coterie of photographers at a groundbreaking LGBT festival. The race
and other games including handbag throwing were some of the ²(   ) of
the "&Proud" festival, which took place in public for the first time in a country where
same-sex relations are still ³(   ) illegal.

A report by the United Nations argues that inequality can hinder poverty reduction, harm economic growth, and
5 exclude people within societies. There has always been inequality in some form or other in every society in all countries. But with two-thirds of global wealth going
10 to the richest 1 percent by 2030 there are questions over why the

gap continues to grow. Inequality can be divided into two groups: outcomes and opportunity.

Inequality of outcomes occurs when a person is economically less well off than
15 another. This might be in income, education, or health. It is related to a person's standard of living. Many believe that the single biggest cause of this inequality is globalization. They argue that gaps between people grow as countries enter world trade and money markets. Studies show how financial rules often favor the few rather than the economic activity of the whole country. Without equality in outcomes,
20 a person is unlikely to gain equality in opportunity.

Inequality of opportunity occurs when a person does not have the same freedom to choose the kind of life they would like to live. This may be due to their gender, ethnicity, or sexual orientation. The lack of opportunity prevents people from using their skills and ideas. They are marginalized and treated unfairly. Once again this
25 results in lower economic growth and increases poverty.

Reducing inequality means bringing about great change in society. More must be invested in health, education, and jobs for all. It also means more inclusive social practices and greater financial protection for those who are disadvantaged.

(259 words)

Notes

marginalized 社会的に無視された   **disadvantaged** 恵まれない人々

1 | Vocabulary Check

Fill in the blanks with the most appropriate words from the list below.

1. Studying abroad is a great (   ) to broaden your horizons.

2. People of a different (   ) may hold different cultural norms.

3. The committee decided against promoting the event due to (   )

   difficulties.

4. Teachers should (   ) every student equally.

5. The major economic depression (   ) Daniel's career.

> financial   hindered   ethnicity   opportunity   treat

2 | Comprehension Questions

Answer the following questions in English.

1. By 2030, what proportion of global wealth is predicted to go to the richest 1 percent?

   ....

2. When does inequality of outcomes occur?

   ....

3. What do many people believe is the biggest cause of inequality of outcomes?

   ....

4. When does inequality of opportunity occur?

   ....

5. What does reducing inequality mean?

   ....

3 | Grammar Check

Unscramble the following words and complete the sentences.

1. [all, every, classes, student, in] decided to participate in the event.

   .... decided to participate in the event.

2. It is still unknown [the, why, suddenly, disappeared, man].

   It is still unknown ....

3. Selena decided to stay in her hometown [state, the, to, than, moving, rather]

    capital.

    Selena decided to stay in her hometown ....

    capital.

▌▌▌ DISCUSSION

Goal 10: REDUCED INEQUALITIES
Why it matters

世界の人口の一部を除外してしまうと、持続可能な開発は達成できません。 そのような状況を避けるため、以下の目標が挙げられています。

Goal	To reduce inequalities within and among countries. （国内外の不平等を減らす）

この目標を達成するために、私たちに何ができるでしょうか？ 以下に挙げる例から自分ができると思う行動を１つ選び、その理由をクラスで発表しましょう。

Daily actions you may want to take:

1. Encourage children to make friends with kids from different cultures.
2. Once a month, have a coffee with a person who is different from you, whether in race, beliefs, culture, or age.
3. Learn to respect all kinds of people who may do things differently than you.
4. Travel the world to learn about different cultures.
5. Read storybooks to children that describe all cultures.
6. Stop stereotypes. Write a blog of short stories that breaks that way of thinking.

番号： _____

理由	
具体的な行動	

Sustainable Cities & Communities

Bike, walk, or use public transportation

全人口の半数に相当する 35 億人が現在、都市部に居住しています。2030 年までには、50 億人に達すると予測されます。そのため、都市部の生活の中で、貧困や気候変動への対策を見出さなければなりません。住み続けられるまちづくりのために、あなたは何ができますか。

ⅠLISTENING

1 Key Word Study | *Before Watching the Video*

Match each word with its definition.

1. adapt   (   )   2. brave   (   )   3. embrace   (   )

4. ensure   (   )   5. intimidate   (   )   6. motivate   (   )

7. rare   (   )   8. scare   (   )   9. scheme   (   )

10. subscribe   (   )

> a. やる気にさせる   b. 適応する   c. 保証する   d. 勇敢な   e. 計画   f. まれな
>
> g. 推進する   h. 怖がらせる   i. 驚かせる   j. 申し込む

2 Listening Practice 1 | *First Viewing*   (Time 01:33) WEB動画 DVD

Watch the news clip and write T if the statement is true or F if it is false.

1. Vladimir Kumov is using gifts to try and motivate Muscovites to use bicycles.

    (   )

2. They offer free fruits, vegetables, sweets, and coupons.   (   )

3. The bicycle is just a mode of transportation.   (   )

4. The bicycle is a symbol of an ecologically responsible lifestyle.   (   )

5. Public bike-sharing will expand next year.   (   )

Listen to the recording and fill in the missing words.

Narrator: Free bananas, sweets, and discounts for those rare Muscovites who head to work by bicycle.

Muscovites モスクワ市民

Vladimir Kumov: Moscow isn't adapted for cycling yet, so we're trying to motivate people with gifts and our good mood ¹( ) ( ) ( ) ( ) ( ) their colleagues in return.

Narrator: One of the main challenges is to ensure cyclists' safety. The number of cycle lanes in Moscow has tripled since 2012 — but only to a total of just 70 km. ²( ) ( ) ( ), but Russia's bike lovers aren't easily intimidated.

Elizaveta and Lyuba: Sometimes we're going in the wrong direction, or we pass where cars can't go — it's very convenient for us. And the most important thing is that we save time ³( ) ( ) ( ) ( ) ( ) ( ).

Narrator: For others, the bike isn't just a mode of transportation, it's a symbol of an ecologically responsible lifestyle. Luiza uses her Instagram account to get her message across.

a mode of transportation
交通手段

Instagram インスタグラム

Luiza: I think I'm very brave and that's why I cycle. ⁴( ) ( ) ( ) ( ) ( ). But for all my friends to switch to a bike, there must be more cycle lanes and routes.

Narrator: Attitudes are changing, though —
more than 200,000 people already
subscribe to ⁵(   )
(   ) (   )
(   ) (   ).

make a push 努力する

That's set to expand next year as the city makes a
push to embrace pedal power.

----

4 | **Comprehension Check** | *Second Viewing*

WEB動画 DVD

Watch the news clip again and answer the following questions in English.

1. What is one of the main challenges?

    ....

2. How has the number of cycle lanes in Moscow changed since 2012?

    ....

3. What does Luiza use to get her message across?

    ....

4. What must happen for more people to switch to bicycles?

    ....

5. How many people have already subscribed to a public bike-sharing scheme?

    ....

5 | **Summary**

2-11

Listen to the recording and complete the summary.

Two years ago, Luiza Nesterova would never have dreamed of cycling to work in
Russia's capital. But now she bikes everywhere, ¹(   ) by busy roads that
are still a battleground for cyclists. To encourage other Muscovites to do the same,
she has ²(   ) an Instagram page that gets viewed more than 5,400 times
per day. She often gets interviewed by Russian media and has become a kind of
³(   ) for cycling.

By 2050, 75 percent of all the people on earth, will live in cities. In Asia, it is thought that cities will grow by more than a billion
5 people in this time. With the high level of growth, cities are struggling to keep up with basic services. There are issues with housing, the supply of power,
10 and poor sanitation. The figures are proving a great challenge for planners and developers who must create the infrastructure for livable cities of the future.

One way they are doing this is by designing sustainable cities. A sustainable city,
15 sometimes called an "ecocity," is planned to have the least social, economic, and environmental impact. They are designed in ways that meet the needs of current and future generations. For those living in the cities they provide safe, low cost housing. Accessible green and public spaces aim to create areas that filter dust and provide cooler, shaded areas. Public transport systems use new technology to
20 protect air quality. And fewer trucks are needed on streets as waste is managed with underground pipes to recycling plants. These actions are used with better risk strategies to build environments that are safer and better able to withstand natural disasters.

In Japan, several cities have chosen to adopt similar energy policies for the future.
25 In Tokyo, the government is promoting the use of zero-emission vehicles and energy-efficient buildings. They plan to halve food waste by 2030 and reduce the amount of single-use plastics in order to protect marine life.

By creating these cities, planners hope to find the right mix of social and economic benefits that will sustain life and ensure the future of the planet.

(277 words)

1 | Vocabulary Check

Fill in the blanks with the most appropriate words from the list below.

1. The police immediately responded to the scene to prevent a further

   (   ).

2. The news reporter updated viewers on the (   ) situation of the

   incident.

3. Smartphones have rapidly become (   ) to the general public over the

   past 10 years.

4. More and more people these days choose to (   ) cats from animal

   shelters.

5. New air conditioners are (   ) to save energy.

   adopt   disaster   current   designed   accessible

2 | Comprehension Questions

Answer the following questions in English.

1. What proportion of all the people on earth will live in cities by 2050?

   ....

2. Given the high level of growth, what issues of basic services are cities struggling

   with?

   ....

3. What is a sustainable city planned to have?

   ....

4. What do public transport systems use in an ecocity?

   ....

5. What is the government promoting in Tokyo?

   ....

3 | Grammar Check

Unscramble the following words and complete the sentences.

1. The population of the town [3 percent, every, year, been, by, has, decreasing]

   over the past decade.

   The population of the town .... over

   the past decade.

71

2. Ms. Miller's students have [to, to, up, with, study, keep, hard] the challenging course materials.

   Ms. Miller's students have .... the challenging course materials.

3. [number, people, shown, have, of, up, a] to watch the movie premier.

   .... to watch the movie premier.

▌▌▌ DISCUSSION

Goal 11: SUSTAINABLE CITIES AND COMMUNITIES
Why it matters

2030 年までに 50 億人が都市部に住むと予測されています。 そのため、以下の目標が挙げられています。

Goal	To make cities inclusive, safe, resilient, and sustainable. (都市を包括的で、安全で、回復力があり、持続可能なものにする)

この目標を達成するために、私たちに何ができるでしょうか？ 以下に挙げる例から自分ができると思う行動を 1 つ選び、その理由をクラスで発表しましょう。

Daily actions you may want to take:

1. Start a car-pooling system online, internally in the office, or in areas that don't have access to reliable public transport.
2. Generate awareness about your city's carbon footprint and ways to improve it.
3. Advocate and support the development of sport and recreational spaces. They help build stronger, healthier, happier, and safer communities.
4. Use public transport, city bikes and other modes of environmentally friendly transport.
5. Educate yourself on the cultural and natural heritage of your area. Visit heritage sites and post about these in a positive light.
6. As a company, offer reduced fees on city bicycle hire.

番号：＿＿＿＿＿

理由	
具体的な行動	

LESSON 12

Responsible Consumption & Production

Recycle paper, plastic, glass, and aluminum

　2050 年までに地球の人口は 96 億人に達すると予測されています。私たちが、生産や消費のパターンを変更しなければ、地球環境に取り返しのつかない大きなダメージを与えると考えられます。使う責任、作る責任として、あなたは何ができますか。

I LISTENING

1 | Key Word Study | Before Watching the Video

Match each word with its definition.

1. appropriate　（　）　2. bale　　　　（　）　3. barrel　　　　（　）

4. comparative　（　）　5. dump　　　（　）　6. infrastructure（　）

7. municipality　（　）　8. persuade　（　）　9. promote　　　（　）

10. struggle　　（　）

a. 推奨する	b. 説得する	c. 悪戦苦闘する	d. 比較の	e. 詰める
f. 基盤施設	g. 投げ捨てる	h. 圧縮梱包した大型荷物	i.（地方自治体の）当局	
j. 適切な				

2 | Listening Practice 1 | First Viewing　　　　(Time 02:40) WEB動画 DVD

Watch the news clip and write T if the statement is true or F if it is false.

1. Trucks dump rubbish at landfills in Cyprus.　　　　　　　　　　（　）

2. Cyprus has the appropriate infrastructure for recycling.　　　　（　）

3. The rubbish baskets are divided for different types of rubbish.　（　）

4. A five-star hotel in Ayia Napa is not willing to promote sustainable tourism.

　　　　　　　　　　　　　　　　　　　　　　　　　　　　　（　）

5. Green-Dot collects and separates paper, glass, metals, and plastics.　（　）

73

Listen to the recording and fill in the missing words.

Narrator : At one of the two landfills serving the Republic of Cyprus, trucks can dump one ton of rubbish for a five-Euro fee. In 2013, the European Commission gave the government two years to close these landfills, but the environment department is struggling to find other solutions to the island's waste.

Costas Hadjopanayiotou: Cyprus nowadays is sending to landfill about 75 percent of the total production of the solid waste management, and
[1](   ) (   ) (   ) (   ) is that the appropriate infrastructure for recycling, separating at source and so on is not in place.

Narrator : Increasing numbers of tourists visiting Cyprus are contributing to the problem. In 2016, more than three million people visited the island, famous for its Mediterranean beaches. In Ayia Napa, one of the most popular seaside resorts, the municipality has installed recycling bins to tackle the issue.

Helen Mikhaylenko: I see the rubbish baskets are
[2](   ) (   ) (   ) (   ) (   ) (   ). It's a very good idea because the rubbish is one of the global problems and it is solved in Ayia Napa in this way. I think it is very good.

Narrator : This five-star hotel in Ayia Napa is trying to promote sustainable tourism. The hotel has cut the level of landfill per guest by half since it began persuading them to sort their rubbish in 2003. But the rising number of tourists makes this increasingly difficult.

Republic of Cyprus
キプロス共和国

European Commission
欧州委員会

in place 環境が整って

contribute to
〜の一因となる

Mediterranean beaches
地中海沿岸の海岸
Ayia Napa キプロス南海岸のリゾート地

Panicos Michael: I think that this will be a big challenge for
the island and in general ³( ) ( )
( ) ( ) ( ) ( )
( ) which is going to be produced.

Narrator : NGO Green-Dot set up the first collecting system on
the island in 2005. They gather and separate paper,
glass, and certain metals and plastics at sorting
plants where they manage some 12 tons of recycled
waste per day. The waste is barreled into bales and
⁴( ) ( ) ( ) ( ).
They say the government is not putting tools in place
to manage waste in a more sustainable way.

Green-Dot (Cyprus)
2005年に設立されたキプロス
のNGO

sorting plant 仕分け工場

put ～ in place ～を制定する

Kyriakos Parpounas: You can see that in the comparative
tables, Cyprus is one of those countries that has
⁵( ) ( ) ( )
( ) ( ) ( ) that
actually help the growth of recycling.

Narrator : The EU wants Cyprus to recycle 50 percent of its
waste by 2020. But with the country reaching just 19
percent, there's still much work to be done.

----

4 | Comprehension Check | *Second Viewing*

WEB動画 DVD

Watch the news clip again and answer the following questions in English.

1. What percentage of the total production of solid waste management is sent to landfill?

   ....

2. How many people visited the island in 2016?

   ....

3. How much landfill has the hotel cut since it began persuading the guests to sort their rubbish in 2003?

   ....

4. How many tons of recycled waste do sorting plants manage per day?

   ....

5. What does the EU want Cyprus to do by 2020?

   ....

5 | Summary

Listen to the recording and complete the summary.

With more visitors heading to Cyprus than ever, the Mediterranean island's waste
¹(   ) system is under pressure, despite efforts to cut landfill use and
encourage recycling, waste management, and tourism. Cyprus has much improved
its ²(   ) management since 2005, when Green Dot was founded in response
to a new European Union law ³(   ) better sorting and recycling.

❚❚ READING

2-16

As the population of the earth increases,
the demands put on natural resources also
rise. Human beings use natural resources
such as water, energy, and food in large
5 quantities every day. But without reducing
the use of resources, future generations will
find life more difficult. There are a number
of simple ways that each person can help cut
demand.

10   Much of the water used in households comes from underground stores. Global
warming and processes such as deforestation mean the stores are not refilling fast
enough to cope with high demand. In developed countries, the average person uses
150 liters of water each day. In order to reduce this amount, simple measures can be
taken. Turning off the tap when brushing teeth, taking shorter showers, or investing
15 in water-efficient goods can make a big difference in the amount being used.

   At current rates, the global use of energy is unsustainable. In 2016, 69 percent of
greenhouse gas emissions from homes were from the use of electricity. The easiest
way to conserve energy is to simply turn off lights and appliances when not using
them. This is particularly important for heating and cooling devices as they use the
20 most energy and produce the highest emissions.

   Even the smallest changes in food choices can be environmentally friendly. One
of the most effective ways of protecting the environment is to eat less meat. Livestock
uses deforested land and releases methane gas that both contribute to climate change.

   By making small changes in our consumption behavior, it is possible to reduce our
25 use of resources and therefore help maintain the future of the environment.

(269 words)

Notes
livestock 家畜

1 | Vocabulary Check

Fill in the blanks with the most appropriate words from the list below.

1. Mainstream potato chips contain a large (　　　　　) of oil.

2. The temperature of Japanese summers may soon become unbearable at this (　　　　　).

3. Animals hibernate to (　　　　　) energy during the cold months.

4. You can bring your own bottles to (　　　　　) tea and coffee.

5. The bald eagle was (　　　　　) back into the wild after treatment.

> quantity　　refill　　conserve　　rate　　released

2 | Comprehension Questions

Answer the following questions in English.

1. What natural resources do human beings use every day?

    ....

2. How much water does an average person use each day in developed countries?

    ....

3. What simple measures can we take to reduce the amount of water use?

    ....

4. What is the easiest way to conserve energy?

    ....

5. What is one of the most effective ways of protecting the environment?

    ....

3 | Grammar Check

Unscramble the following words and complete the sentences.

1. Many tourists [find, attractive, an, Japan, country] to visit.

    Many tourists .... to visit.

2. Ms. Williams [enough, to, early, made, money, retire].

    Ms. Williams ....

3. Small actions in our daily life [make, can, in, a, the, big, future, difference].

    Small actions in our daily life ....

77

Goal 12: RESPONSIBLE CONSUMPTION AND PRODUCTION
Why it matters

2050 年までに世界の人口が 96 億人に達すると、現在の生活様式を維持するためには、地球約 3 つに相当するものが必要になります。 そのような状況を避けるため、以下の目標が挙げられています。

Goal	To ensure sustainable consumption and production patterns. (持続可能な消費と生産パターンを確保する)

この目標を達成するために、私たちに何ができるでしょうか？ 以下に挙げる例から自分ができると思う行動を 1 つ選び、その理由をクラスで発表しましょう。

Daily actions you may want to take:

1. Don't keep clothes or other items you are not using. Donate them.
2. Buy fruit that is oddly shaped and overripe, and make smoothies out of it.
3. Recycle!
4. Keep showers short. Don't fill the bath to the top. Excessive use of water contributes to global water stress.
5. Buy sustainable products including electronics, toys, shampoo, seafood, and organic groceries.
6. Eat local. And support fair-trade associations that support and promote businesses committed to the principles of fair-trade.

番号：＿＿＿＿＿

理由	
具体的な行動	

LESSON 13 — Climate Action

Educate young people on climate change

　気候変動は、人間の活動によって引き起こされ、私たちの地球の未来を脅かしています。パリ協定は、地球環境にやさしい産業への投資市場に、23 兆ドルのビジネス機会をもたらしました。気候変動に具体的な対策として、あなたは何ができますか。

❶ LISTENING

1 | Key Word Study | *Before Watching the Video*

Match each word with its definition.

1. architectural　(　)　　2. autonomous　(　)　　3. deteriorate　(　)

4. devote　　　　(　)　　5. disgrace　　　(　)　　6. fund　　　　　(　)

7. idiot　　　　　(　)　　8. integral　　　　(　)　　9.self-sufficient　(　)

10. sewage　　　 (　)

a. 愚か者	b. 不名誉	c. 専念させる	d. 悪化する	e. 自律した
f. 建築学の	g. なくてはならない	h. 下水	i. 資金を出す	j. 自給自足できる

2 | Listening Practice 1 | *First Viewing*　　　　　　　(Time 02:14) WEB動画 🖥 💿DVD

Watch the news clip and write T if the statement is true or F if it is false.

1. This is the only sustainable school in South America.　　　　　(　)

2. The school building uses sun and rain as energy sources.　　　 (　)

3. A local NGO helped design the school building.　　　　　　　 (　)

4. The students learn about sustainable living.　　　　　　　　　(　)

5. The students collect glass and plastic for recycling.　　　　　　(　)

79

Listen to the recording and fill in the missing words.

Narrator: A sunny winter's day is great news for these Uruguayan children. As pupils of South America's first sustainable school, they study in a building heated  only using solar panels. On top of the normal school program they learn about recycling, energy saving, and growing their own food.

Uruguayan ウルグアイの

Francesco Fassina: The school is an autonomous building in the sense that it isn't connected to any energy infrastructure for water or anything. It's sustainable ¹( ) ( ) ( ) ( ) ( ). Totally autonomous, and it works thanks to its connection with nature: the sun and the rain.

thanks to 〜のおかげで

Narrator: The building was funded by a local NGO and a detergent company and designed by US architect Michael Reynolds, a self-professed "garbage warrior" who has devoted his career to building self-sufficient structures out of recyclable material.

self-professed 自称
garbage warrior ごみ戦士

Michael Reynolds: People called me an idiot: building with garbage, what a fool, you're a disgrace to the architectural community. You know, I was trying to  contain sewage and treat it and ²( ) ( ) ( ) ( ) ( ) that architects didn't do.

Narrator: The 39 students, some just starting preschool and others in their final year before university, learn it's possible to live in a building ³( ) ( ) ( ) ( ). NGO volunteers organize regular workshops on sustainability… for pupils… and teachers too.

Alicia Alvarez: Little by little, we are becoming qualified, in fact we are being trained by them. We are being trained to learn how the school works, how to maintain it, so that the systems don't deteriorate.

Narrator : Some of the children have even [4]( ) ( ) ( ) ( ).

Danila Mendez: Every day, we walk here and he finds glass in the sand, or plastic or something, and he picks it up. He says I'm keeping this to throw it away… He doesn't leave it there. He picks it up and he [5]( ) ( ) ( ) ( ) ( ) ( ) ( ).

Narrator : For these little garbage warriors, saving the planet has become an integral part of their homework.

---

4 | Comprehension Check | *Second Viewing*

WEB動画 DVD

Watch the news clip again and answer the following questions in English.

1. How is the building heated?

   ....

2. Why is the school called an autonomous building?

   ....

3. What does Michael Reynolds do?

   ....

4. What do NGO volunteers organize?

   ....

5. What has become an integral part of the students' homework?

   ....

5 | Summary

Listen to the recording and complete the summary.

A building made of tires and glass and plastic bottles, off the ¹( ) and non-polluting: a village in Uruguay is home to a fully sustainable school — and a bold ²( ) in green citizenship. The school is a good example: It produces no waste and, across from the three ³( ), the compost-fed kitchen garden brims with basil, tomatoes, strawberries, and chard.

▌▌ READING

 2-20

The earth's climate has always changed. The difference now is that the change is faster. This is not a natural change, but the result of human actions. Greenhouse
5 gases are released when fossil fuels are used as energy. Once in the atmosphere, the trapped gases reflect sunlight back to the earth, warming the planet. If no action is taken to reduce the trapped heat, global
10 temperatures will increase and negatively impact the ecosystem.

To achieve a sustainable future, action needs to be taken to lower emissions. Developing countries are in most need of help. Local people continue to use traditional sources of energy such as firewood, charcoal, or animal waste. On a national level,
15 newly industrializing nations are using cheap energy sources such as coal. The international community must take steps to offer new sources of energy that are more efficient. Unfortunately, this is more expensive, and many developing countries have little choice but to continue with fossil fuels. Therefore, developed countries need to offer more financial support to allow renewable energy companies to compete. At
20 the same time, research and development could look for ways to adapt technology to local areas. However, past projects have had a number of problems. Some caused unintended damage to the environment, while others went ahead without consulting local communities. This led to distrust, and major changes have yet to be realized.

Clearly, to combat the effects of climate change, there must be action. Climate
25 change will affect every person, and so the international community must do all it can to help those who need it.

(263 words)

1 Vocabulary Check

Fill in the blanks with the most appropriate words from the list below.

1. The board of directors decided to (   ) an outside party about the issue.

2. Michael's action had (   ) consequences.

3. Athletes from all over the world gather and (   ) at the Olympics.

4. The (   ) of this school encourages students' learning.

5. Could you adjust the (   ) of this classroom?

> unintended   compete   consult   temperature   atmosphere

2 Comprehension Questions

Answer the following questions in English.

1. How is climate change different from before?

   ....

2. How do greenhouse gases warm the planet?

   ....

3. What sources of energy do local people in developing countries continue to use?

   ....

4. What does the international community have to do?

   ....

5. What problems have past projects had?

   ....

3 Grammar Check

Unscramble the following words and complete the sentences.

1. The thieves [being, are, chased, the, by, police].

   The thieves ....

2. [little, has, there, rain, been] in the area this summer.

   .... in the area this summer.

3. Countries are [energy, sources, alternative, of, for, looking].

   Countries are ....

 **DISCUSSION**

Goal 13: CLIMATE ACTION
Why it matters

パリ協定は、温暖化防止に貢献する投資のために、新興市場で23兆ドル近くのビジネスチャンスを開拓するのに貢献しています。 そのため、以下の目標が挙げられています。

Goal	Taking urgent action to tackle climate change and its impacts. (気候変動とその影響に取り組むための迅速な行動をとる)

この目標を達成するために、私たちに何ができるでしょうか？ 以下に挙げる例から自分ができると思う行動を1つ選び、その理由をクラスで発表しましょう。

Daily actions you may want to take:

1. Compost food scraps.
2. Take reuseable bags to the store.
3. Air-dry. Let your hair and clothes dry naturally.
4. Organize for your school or company to plant new trees every year. Trees release oxygen and take in carbon dioxide.
5. Unplug TVs, computers, and other electronics when not in use.
6. Only buy what you need. 20-50 percent of the food we buy ends up in landfill.

番号：＿＿＿＿＿＿

理由	
具体的な行動	

Life Below Water

Avoid plastic bags to keep the ocean safe and clean

　30億以上の人が、生活のために海の生物多様性に依存しています。海は、食料、薬、バイオ燃料など、重要な天然資源を提供してくれます。きれいな海を保つことは、気候変動の対策にもなります。海をきれいにするために、あなたは何ができますか。

ⅠLISTENING

1 | Key Word Study | *Before Watching the Video*

Match each word with its definition.

1. abundantly   (   )   2. archipelago   (   )   3. biodegradable   (   )

4. consume   (   )   5. conventional   (   )   6. deter   (   )

7. discard   (   )   8. dissolve   (   )   9.diverse   (   )

10. equivalent   (   )

a. 摂取する	b. 豊富に	c. 廃棄する	d. 思いとどまらせる	e. 多様な
f. 分解する	g. 相当する	h. 従来型の	i. 生物分解可能な	j. 群島

2 | Listening Practice 1 | *First Viewing*   (Time 01:56) WEB動画 DVD

Watch the news clip and write T if the statement is true or F if it is false.

1. Cassava is a tropical root rarely found in Indonesia.   (   )
2. Bags made from cassava are not eco-friendly or safe.   (   )
3. Indonesia comes second in terms of marine littering.   (   )
4. The population of Indonesia is about 255 million.   (   )
5. Indonesia's government now has some funding to reduce plastic waste.   (   )

Listen to the recording and fill in the missing words.

Narrator : You can burn it — you can even drink it. This carrier bag was not made with plastic, but with cassava — a tropical root found abundantly in Indonesia.

cassava キャッサバ、イモノキ

Kevin Kumala: Our bags are so eco-friendly that it has passed oral toxicity tests, in which it is totally harmless for animals to consume it. So me drinking it is just to show you that ¹( ) ( ) ( ) ( ) and it gives you hope for these sea animals.

oral toxicity test 経口毒性試験

Narrator : Indonesia is facing a plastic waste crisis driven by years of economic growth in one of the world's most diverse ecosystems. ²( ) ( ) ( ) ( ) marine littering, the archipelago of over 17,000 islands is the world's number two, after China, according to a study.

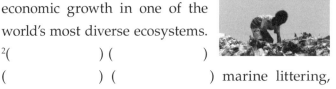

Kevin Kumala: Just in Indonesia alone, a country with a population of 255 million people — if you're talking about straws alone, we're talking about 255 million people times 20 centimeters of plastic straw being discarded every single day. That is 5,000 kilometers of plastic being discarded on a daily basis, and ³( ) ( ) ( ) ( ) ( ) ( ) ( ) Jakarta to Sydney.

Narrator : Unlike the years needed for conventional plastic, most of these biodegradable products can ⁴( ) ( ) ( ) ( )( ) ( ) ( ). But it all comes at a

come at a price 高く付く

price. A cassava bag costs nearly twice the price of its artificial counterpart — which so far has deterred consumers in Southeast Asia's largest market.

artificial counterpart
人工の同等のもの

Tuti Hendrawati Mintarsih: But if the market in Indonesia increases, then
⁵(   ) (   )
(   ) (   )
(   ) for Indonesia and also the price of the plastic will also be cheaper.

Narrator : Indonesia currently has no government funding aimed at reducing plastic waste. But despite many challenges, the hopes of its small bio-producers are unlikely to easily dissolve.

bio-producers
バイオ燃料の生産業者

---

4 | Comprehension Check | *Second Viewing*

WEB動画 DVD

Watch the news clip again and answer the following questions in English.

1. In what way are the bags from cassava eco-friendly?

....

2. What problem is Indonesia facing due to economic growth?

....

3. What is the total length of plastic straws discarded per day?

....

4. How long does it take for cassava plastic products to break down?

....

5. Why don't consumers in Indonesia want to use cassava bags?

....

5 | Summary

 2-23

Listen to the recording and complete the summary.

From bags washing up on Bali's beaches to food packaging scattered across roads and
¹(   ) waterways in cities, Indonesia is facing a plastic waste crisis driven by years of ²(   ) economic growth. An entrepreneur from Bali, disgusted at the rubbish littering the famous holiday island, is trying to tackle the problem with
³(   ) to conventional plastic.

Eighty percent of life on earth lives in the oceans. For human beings the oceans provide 50 percent of our oxygen and absorb 30 percent of CO_2. They are fundamental to communities for food, work, and leisure. So why do we do so much damage to them?

In the Pacific Ocean, there is an area made up of 100 million tons of debris. It mainly contains plastics brought together by currents and winds. Every piece of scrap plastic in streams and rivers will likely find its way to the oceans. The plastic can sink to the ocean floor damaging corals and habitats, or float near the surface. Fish that swallow the plastic die or are eaten and pass the plastic on into the food chain. Nothing can change this, but further damage can be slowed by avoiding using plastic in the first place, reusing it, or recycling it.

It is claimed that by 2048 all the species fished today will be extinct. Overfishing occurs when more fish are caught than can reproduce and repopulate the stock. Some reasons for this are: unregulated or unreported fishing, having unprotected areas, or allowing too many fishing boats. Overfishing larger predators removes them from the oceans and increases the number of smaller creatures that remain. These creatures can cause fatal damage to coral reefs and the ecosystem. Without predators, algae grows in uncontrolled amounts taking light from the surviving fish below it. Local communities that rely on fishing on a small scale can lose their food and their livelihoods.

Unless something is done to slow down human threats from plastic and overfishing, it seems likely that the entire ecosystem will one day be damaged beyond repair.

(279 words)

Notes

debris がれき、堆積物

1 Vocabulary Check

Fill in the blanks with the most appropriate words from the list below.

1. Freedom of speech is a (   ) right in a democratic society.

2. Sponges can (   ) moisture in the air.

3. Many species of animals have become (   ) in the past century.

4. Feral cats have become a major (   ) of indigenous species in New Zealand.

5. Australian bushland is the (   ) of koalas.

absorb	fundamental	habitat	extinct	predator

2 Comprehension Questions

Answer the following questions in English.

1. How much life on earth lives in the ocean?

   ....

2. What does debris in the Pacific Ocean contain?

   ....

3. How can we slow further damage by plastic to the oceans?

   ....

4. Why does overfishing occur?

   ....

5. How does overfishing affect local communities that rely on fishing on a small scale?

   ....

3 Grammar Check

Unscramble the following words and complete the sentences.

1. The number of tourists to Japan [continue, increase, likely, is, to, to].

   The number of tourists to Japan ....

2. I will go first [the, in, up, unless, next, shows, Jessica] five minutes.

   I will go first .... five minutes.

3. An iceberg hides nearly 90 percent of [surface, mass, the, its, below].

   An iceberg hides nearly 90 percent of ....

Goal 14: LIFE BELOW WATER
Why it matters

30 億人以上の人々が生活のために海洋と沿岸の生物多様性に依存しています。 そのため、以下の目標が挙げられています。

Goal	To conserve and sustainably use the world's oceans, seas, and marine resources. (世界の海洋、海岸、そして海洋資源を保護し、持続可能に利用する)

この目標を達成するために、私たちに何ができるでしょうか？ 以下に挙げる例から自分ができると思う行動を１つ選び、その理由をクラスで発表しましょう。

To conserve and sustainably use the world's oceans, seas and marine resources.

Daily actions you may want to take:

1. Start regularly volunteering in community groups to clean up a portion of the beach from litter if you live nearby.
2. Eat local sustainable food.
3. Support organizations that protect the oceans.
4. Use fewer plastic products, which often end up in oceans causing the death of marine animals.
5. Avoid buying wild-caught, salt-water fish for your home aquarium.
6. Only use the dishwasher and washing machine when they are full.

番号：＿＿＿＿＿

理由	
具体的な行動	

LESSON 15

Life on Land

Plant a tree and help protect the environment

地球の陸地の約 31％は森林です。7000 万人の原住民を含む 16 億人が、生活を森林に依存しています。呼吸をする空気、飲む水、食べる食料など、森林が私たちを支えています。陸の豊かさを守るために、あなたは何ができますか。

I LISTENING

1 | Key Word Study | *Before Watching the Video*

Match each word with its definition.

1. captive   (   )   2. clash   (   )   3. confrontation (   )

4. endangered   (   )   5. intensify   (   )   6. mitigate   (   )

7. objective   (   )   8. roam   (   )   9. settlement   (   )

10. a squad of (   )

a. 目的	b. 対立	c. 開拓地	d. うろつく	e. 絶滅寸前の
f. 増大する	g. 捕らわれの	h. ～隊、チーム	i. 衝突	j. 軽減する

2 | Listening Practice 1 | *First Viewing* (Time 01:51) WEB動画 🖥 DVD

Watch the news clip and write T if the statement is true or F if it is false.

1. Eko Arianto is a park ranger in Sumatra, Indonesia.   (   )

2. The park rangers' job is to keep elephants away from human habitats.   (   )

3. Sumatran elephants are very important for the future.   (   )

4. Sumatran elephants are an endangered species that must be protected.   (   )

5. Park ranger patrols are not successful and human-elephant clashes have
   increased.   (   )

Listen to the recording and fill in the missing words.

Narrator : Following trails deep into the forest — until finally one is spotted: Indonesia's Sumatran elephant. ¹( ) ( ) ( ) ( ) these animals and human settlements is a round-the-clock job for these park rangers.

Indonesia's Sumatran elephant インドネシアのスマトラ象

round-the-clock 24時間体制の

Eko Arianto: The primary objective of ²( ) ( ) ( ) ( ) is to mitigate human-animal conflict, using our elephants.

Narrator : Confrontations between elephants and humans can quickly turn violent in Sumatra, where competition for space has intensified ³( ) ( ) ( ) ( ) of natural habitat. The World Wildlife Fund says nearly 70 percent of the Sumatran elephants' ecosystem has been destroyed in a single generation. In 2012 the species was declared critically endangered.

The World Wildlife Fund 世界自然保護基金

Eko Arianto: Sumatran elephants are an icon. It's very important for the future of this endangered species that ⁴( ) ( ) ( ). If the community feels involved, then they will protect them.

Narrator : Response units like this one are located throughout Way Kambas National Park, where an estimated 250 wild Sumatran elephants still roam today. The rangers use a squad of six captive elephants

Way Kambas National Park ウェイカンバス国立公園

to patrol the park's borders,
5( ) ( )
( ) ( )
( ) that could put the
wild animals at risk. Estimating
an 80 percent drop in human-elephant clashes since
the patrolling began in 2015 — these response units
have proved successful and may hold the key for the
future survival of these iconic animals.

iconic 象徴的な

---

4 | Comprehension Check | *Second Viewing*

Watch the news clip again and answer the following questions in English.

1. What is a park rangers' job in Sumatran national parks?

....

2. Why do confrontations between elephants and humans turn violent?

....

3. What does the World Wildlife Fund say about the Sumatran elephants?

....

4. How many elephants are estimated to live in the Way Kambas National Park today?

....

5. By what percentage have human-elephant clashes dropped since the patrolling began in 2015?

....

5 | Summary

2-27

Listen to the recording and complete the summary.

Confrontations between elephants and humans can quickly turn violent in Sumatra, where competition for space has 1( ) as the island's forests have been rapidly cleared for timber and farming. Their 2( ) has paid off. Rangers estimate the frequency of clashes has dropped up to 80 percent since they began 3( ) the area in 2015.

In 2017, 7,900 square kilometers of the Amazon forest was permanently cut down and cleared. That is

5 an area almost three and a half times the size of Tokyo. The Amazon is the largest and most biodiverse tropical rainforest on earth.

10 It absorbs large amounts of carbon dioxide and produces 20 percent of the air that we breathe. However, over time large areas of tree cover are being destroyed for other uses.

15 One of the biggest threats to the Amazon is logging. Trees are cleared for roads, ranches, and farms for activities such as grazing cattle or growing soybeans. Moreover, felled trees are burned for charcoal that drives industrial production. The loss of so many trees is thought to be a factor in climate change. Trees not only store large amounts of carbon dioxide; they also release it into the air when they die.

20 And the loss of trees has further effects. More than half of the 10 million species of plants, animals, and insects live in the Amazon. Without trees they lose their natural habitat, and many species are near extinction. The loss of plants is a problem for the companies that use them to create many of the most common medicines. Trees may be replaced by planting new trees, however, this does not solve all the problems.

25 Species that are dying out may not be able to recover, nor will it help with the levels of greenhouse gases previously emitted.

The loss of forests and their species will be disastrous for the earth. It will take strong international cooperation to challenge current trends and implement solutions to protect one of the world's natural wonders. (276 words)

30

Notes

ranch 牧場　**graze** 草を食べる

1 | Vocabulary Check

Fill in the blanks with the most appropriate words from the list below.

1. The head of the committee was (   ) after an allegation of bribery.
2. This documentary illustrates some (   ) events of the 20th century.
3. The legendary treasure is said to have been hidden in a cave (   )
4. (   ) such as price, distance, and weather affect people's decision on travel destinations.
5. Chocolate should be (   ) in a cool, dry place.

> factors   disastrous   replaced   stored   permanently

2 | Comprehension Questions

Answer the following questions in English.

1. How many square kilometers of the Amazon forest was permanently cut down and cleared in 2017?

   ....

2. How much of the air that we breathe does the Amazon produce?

   ....

3. What is one of the biggest threats to the Amazon?

   ....

4. What proportion of species of plants, animals, and insects lives in the Amazon?

   ....

5. For what kind of companies is the loss of plants a problem?

   ....

3 | Grammar Check

Unscramble the following words and complete the sentences.

1. Capybaras are [of, the, rodents, species, biggest] in the world.

   Capybaras are .... in the world.

2. Cheetahs can run [than, a, and, one, times, half, faster] tigers.

   Cheetahs can run .... tigers.

3. Lack of time [why, reasons, of, was, the, one] Jamie did not join the fieldwork.

   Lack of time .... Jamie did not join the fieldwork.

Goal 15: LIFE ON LAND
Why it matters

約 16 億人が生計を立てるために森林に依存しており、そのうち 7,000 万人が先住民族です。そのため、以下の目標が挙げられています。

Goal	To sustainably manage forests, combat desertification, halt and reverse land degradation, and halt biodiversity loss. （持続可能な方法で森林を管理し、砂漠化と闘い、土地の劣化を止め、回復させ、そして生物多様性の喪失を止める）

この目標を達成するために、私たちに何ができるでしょうか？　以下に挙げる例から自分ができると思う行動を 1 つ選び、その理由をクラスで発表しましょう。

Daily actions you may want to take:

1. Eat seasonal produce. It tastes better, it is cheaper and it is environmentally friendly.
2. Never buy products made from threatened or endangered species.
3. Recycle used paper and go paperless where possible.
4. When you go into stores, or when you participate in market places, make environmentally-friendly choices that will benefit our planet.
5. Eat less meat. The production and distribution of meat has a huge impact on greenhouse gas emissions.
6. Buy recycled products.

番号：＿＿＿＿＿

理由	
具体的な行動	

Use your right to elect the leaders

平和で、公正で、非排他的な社会が、持続可能な開発目標を達成するために不可欠です。人々は恐怖や暴力から解放され、安全に暮らすことが保証されるべきです。平和と公正をすべての人にもたらすために、あなたは何ができますか。

Ⅰ LISTENING

1 | Key Word Study | *Before Watching the Video*

Match each word with its definition.

1. apathetic   (   )   2. constituency   (   )   3. convince   (   )

4. demographic   (   )   5. encourage   (   )   6. enormously   (   )

7. participation   (   )   8. profound   (   )   9. rally   (   )

10. referendum   (   )

a. 有権者	b. 呼び集める	c. 膨大に	d. 参加	e. (年齢) 層
f. 心の底からの	g. 〜するように勧める	h. 国民投票	i. 冷淡な	j. 説得する

2 | Listening Practice 1 | *First Viewing*   (Time 01:44) WEB動画 DVD

Watch the news clip and write T if the statement is true or F if it is false.

1. Helen Hayes is a Labor party Member of Parliament.   (   )
2. She would not like young British people to participate in the elections.   (   )
3. Britain has the lowest election participation rates in Europe.   (   )
4. Young people think their voice does not matter to the government.   (   )
5. More younger people than older people will probably turn out in the election on Tuesday.   (   )

Listen to the recording and fill in the missing words.

Narrator : Young Brits have one of the lowest election participation rates in Europe and here in South London, Labor party MP Helen Hayes is trying to change all of that. But it's no easy task.

Labor party 労働党
MP (Member of Parliament) （英）下院議員、国会議員

Helen Hayes: What I've picked up on in this constituency is a profound sense of anger and frustration on the part of young people who weren't able to vote in the EU referendum and a profound sense — [1]( ) ( ) ( ) ( ) ( ) — that the EU referendum is about their future.

Narrator : On average, fewer than 20 percent of under-25s vote in local and European elections in the UK — the lowest rate [2]( ) ( ) ( ) ( ) ( ) in the EU. But that's not to say that all are apathetic about the future of British politics.

Oisín Challen Flynn: You know since the last election, we've had uni fees ramped up enormously, [3]( ) ( ) ( ), ( ) ( ) ( ) ( ), community care, … I think there's a whole lot to play for in this election.

uni fee (university fee) 大学の学費
rack up 値上げする

Narrator : A number of organizations to rally this key demographic have been set up. UpRising uses social media [4]( ) ( ) ( ) ( ) ( ) ( ) and encourage them to attend

UpRising 英国青少年指導力育成団体

workshops like this one.

Gabriela Bossman: I think that because of what's going on young people are actually becoming more politically active. We're realizing that our voice does matter.

Narrator : But others are harder to convince.

Marlon : I don't think my voice can actually be heard because I'm one person. [5](   ) (   ) (   ) (   ) (   ): Conservatives will win so I don't think my voice will make a difference to be honest.

conservatives 保守系の人

Narrator : With only 40 percent of under 25s expected to turn out in Thursday's election compared with 75 percent of over 65s — the future may well be in the hands of the UK's older generation, rather than the younger one.

----

4 | Comprehension Check | *Second Viewing*

WEB動画   DVD

Watch the news clip again and answer the following questions in English.

1. What feeling has Helen Hayes picked up on among young British people?

   ....

2. What is the average percentage of voters in elections among young Brits?

   ....

3. What does Gabriela Bossman think of young people?

   ....

4. Why does Marlon not want to vote in the election?

   ....

5. What percentage of young people under 25 are expected to vote on Tuesday?

   ....

Listen to the recording and complete the summary.

Just a year after the Brexit referendum, Britons return to the polls on June 8 for parliamentary ¹( ). Young voters could play a key role in the outcome, but will they ²( ) to have their voices heard? With only 40 percent of under 25s expected to turn out in Thursday's election compared with 75 percent of over 65s — the future may be in the ³( ) of the UK's older generation, rather than the younger.

II READING

2-32

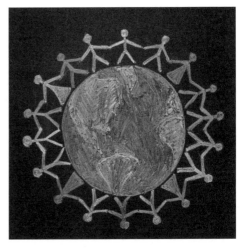

The United Nations was formed in 1945. Its purpose was to maintain peace in all parts of the world. It does this by bringing rival nations together to talk. Although it is not always
5 successful, it makes great efforts to keep the peace between states. In recent years, however, there have been fewer global disputes, but an increase in conflicts within countries. As a result of violence, abuse, or lack of human
10 rights over 65 million people have been forced from their homes. These actions have had adverse effects on economies, and the number of poor people in those states has risen. The UN estimates that the cost of aid will be 50 billion dollars by 2030. Many of the displaced take short-term shelter in countries that face challenges themselves,
15 thereby adding to the poverty and hardship.

Figures show that states with less gender inequality are the least likely to be in conflict. This suggests that allowing more women into jobs with real control will promote peace. It is also clear that financial help must be adapted to encourage more accountable and inclusive institutions. By sharing power amongst all members of
20 society across all communities, it is more likely that progress can occur. Equal rights and inclusive decision making are shown to reduce the number of poor and create the right conditions for long-term sustainable development.

It is important that countries continue to work with each other on the causes of conflict. At the national level, more help must be given to those who work towards
25 more inclusive approaches. In this way, communities can fight for justice, give a voice to every person, and promote peace. (276 words)

1 | Vocabulary Check

Fill in the blanks with the most appropriate words from the list below.

1. Domestic (   ) have been on the rise in some countries.

2. Community leaders vowed to overcome the (   ) together.

3. Some of the spending by the group was not fully (   ).

4. There are numerous academic (   ) in the world.

5. The (   ) weather conditions prevented the hikers from reaching the peak.

accountable   disputes   hardship   adverse   institutions

2 | Comprehension Questions

Answer the following questions in English.

1. When was the United Nations formed?

    ....

2. What has been on the increase in recent years?

    ....

3. How much does the UN estimate the cost of aid will be by 2030?

    ....

4. What do figures show about states with less gender inequality?

    ....

5. What do equal rights and inclusive decision making reduce?

    ....

3 | Grammar Check

Unscramble the following words and complete the sentences.

1. [the, is, although, work, environment, competitive], Wendy enjoys working at the technology company.

    .... , Wendy enjoys working at the technology company.

2. Raymond won first place in the game [as, of, a, work, result, hard].

    Raymond won first place in the game ....

101

3. The strong wind [difficulty, landing, added, of, to, the] at a small airport.

The strong wind .... at a small airport.

III DISCUSSION

Goal 16: PEACE, JUSTICE AND STRONG INSTITUTIONS
Why it matters

持続可能な開発目標を達成するためには、平和で公正かつ包括的な社会が必要です。 そのため、以下の目標が挙げられています。

Goal	Promote peaceful and inclusive societies for sustainable development, provide access to justice for all and build effective, accountable, and inclusive institutions at all levels. (持続可能な開発のために平和で包括的な社会を推進し、すべての人に正義へのアクセスを提供し、あらゆるレベルで効果的で説明がある、包括的な制度を構築する)

この目標を達成するために、私たちに何ができるでしょうか？ 以下に挙げる例から自分ができると思う行動を１つ選び、その理由をクラスで発表しましょう。

Daily actions you may want to take:

1. Make your voice heard and vote in your country's elections.
2. Participate in your country's decision-making processes in an informed manner.
3. Stop violence against women. If you see it happening, report it.
4. Find value in different demographics, thoughts, and beliefs for an inclusive society.
5. Be passionate about your country's decisions, and remain peaceful when standing up for what you believe in.
6. Volunteer at local anti-violence organizations and outreach programs.

番号：＿＿＿＿＿

理由	
具体的な行動	

Web動画のご案内 **StreamLine**

本テキストの映像は、オンラインでのストリーミング再生になります。下記URLよりご利用ください。なお**有効期限は、はじめてログインした時点から1年半**です。

http://st.seibido.co.jp

①

ログイン画面

🔒 LOGIN

テキストに添付されているシールをはがして、12桁のアクセスコードをご入力ください。

[ ] - [ ] - [ ]

同意してログイン

以下の「利用規約」をご確認頂き、同意する場合は上記ボタン【同意してログイン】を押してください。

利用規約

1. このウェブサイト（以下「本サイト」といいます）は、株式会社成美堂（以下「弊社」といいます）が運営しています。弊社の商品・サービス（以下「本サービス」といいます）利用時の会員登録の有無を問わず、本サイトの利用にあたっては、以下のご利用条件をお読み頂き、これらの条件にご同意の上ご利用ください。

2. 本サービスに関して個別に利用規約がある場合、本規約に加えそれらも適用されます。

3. 本サイトを通じて、弊社の商品を販売する第三者のウェブサイトにご案内ないしリンクされることがあります。リンク先ウェブサイトにおいて提供された個人情報は

> 巻末に添付されているシールをはがして、アクセスコードをご入力ください。

②

メニュー画面

AFP World Focus
−Environment, Health, and Technology−
アクセスコード有効期限：2018年4月30日

| 🎬 Video | 🎵 Audio |

Lesson 1: Global Warming and Climat... >
Lesson 2: Diet and Health for Long ... >
Lesson 3: Self-Driving for the Futu... >
Lesson 4: Sustaining Biodiversity a... >
Lesson 5: 3D Printers for Creating ... >
Lesson 6: IT and Education >
Lesson 7: Protection from Natural D... >
Lesson 8: Practical Uses of Drones ... >

> 「Video」または「Audio」を選択すると、それぞれストリーミング再生ができます。

③

再生画面

AFP World Focus
−Environment, Health, and Technology−
アクセスコード有効期限：2018年4月30日

Lesson 2:
Diet and Health for Long Lives
食習慣：長生きのためのスーパーフードを探す

推奨動作環境

【PC OS】
Windows 7~ / Mac 10.8~

【Mobile OS】
iOS / Android ※Android の場合は4.x~が推奨

【Desktop ブラウザ】
Internet Explorer 9~ / Firefox / Chrome / Safari

LINGUAPORTA

リンガポルタのご案内

> **リンガポルタ連動テキストをご購入の学生さんは、「リンガポルタ」を無料でご利用いただけます！**

　本テキストで学習していただく内容に準拠した問題を、オンライン学習システム「リンガポルタ」で学習していただくことができます。PCだけでなく、スマートフォンやタブレットでも学習できます。単語や文法、リスニング力などをよりしっかり身に付けていただくため、ぜひ積極的に活用してください。

　リンガポルタの利用にはアカウントとアクセスコードの登録が必要です。登録方法については下記ページにアクセスしてください。

https://www.seibido.co.jp/linguaporta/register.html

本テキスト「AFPニュースで見る世界 5」のアクセスコードは下記です。

7211-2044-1231-0365-0003-0065-AW87-FSF3

・リンガポルタの学習機能（画像はサンプルです。また、すべてのテキストに以下の4つの機能が用意されているわけではありません）

●多肢選択

●空所補充（音声を使っての聞き取り問題も可能）

●単語並びかえ（マウスや手で単語を移動）

●マッチング（マウスや手で単語を移動）

TEXT PRODUCTION STAFF

edited by	編集
Minako Hagiwara	萩原 美奈子
Takashi Kudo	工藤 隆志

cover design by	表紙デザイン
Ruben Frosali	ルーベン・フロサリ

text design by	本文デザイン
Ruben Frosali	ルーベ ン・フロサリ

CD PRODUCTION STAFF

recorded by	吹き込み者
Rachel Walzer (AmE)	レイチェル・ワルザー（アメリカ英語）
Karen Haedrich (AmE)	カレン・ヘドリック（アメリカ英語）
Dominic Allen (AmE)	ドミニク・アレン（アメリカ英語）
Jack Merluzzi (AmE)	ジャック・マルージ（アメリカ英語）

AFP World News Report 5
—Achieving the Sustainable Development Goals (SDGs)—
AFPニュースで見る世界 5

2020年 1 月20日　初版発行
2023年 2 月25日　第 5 刷発行

著　者　宍戸 真
　　　　Kevin Murphy
　　　　高橋 真理子

発 行 者　佐野 英一郎

発 行 所　株式会社 成 美 堂
　　　　〒101-0052　東京都千代田区神田小川町3-22
　　　　TEL 03-3291-2261　FAX 03-3293-5490
　　　　https://www.seibido.co.jp

印 刷・製 本　三美印刷株式会社

ISBN 978-4-7919-7211-1　　　　　　　　　Printed in Japan